thakali kathakali kathakali

BY CLIFFORD R. JONES AND BETTY TRUE JONES

TRODUCTION TO THE DANCE DRAMA OF KERALA

PHOTO/DESIGN JAN STEWARD

കഥകളി

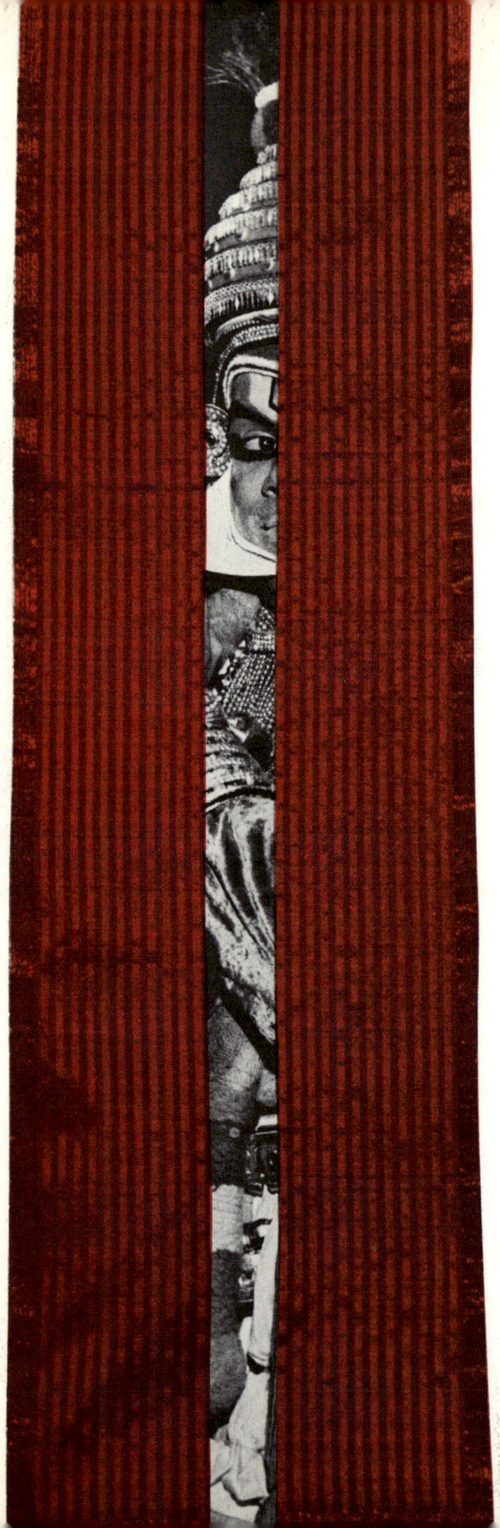

kathakali

AN INTRODUCTION TO THE
DANCE-DRAMA OF KERALA

by
CLIFFORD R. JONES
and
BETTY TRUE JONES

Designed by
JAN STEWARD

The American Society
for Eastern Arts
and
Theatre Arts Books

Prepared for the occasion of the Kerala Kalamandalam Kathakali Company tour of the United States and Canada, under the sponsorship of the American Society for Eastern Arts, San Francisco.

Published by the American Society for Eastern Arts, 405 Sansome Street, San Francisco, and Theatre Arts Books, 333 Sixth Avenue, New York 10014.

First edition, 1970.

Library of Congress Catalog Card Number 70-131488

Printed by the Artisan Press, Los Angeles.

r intent in the publication, Kathakaḷi, An Introduction to ; Dance-Drama of Kerala, is to make available to the nstantly growing audience interested in the performing s of India a simple introductory guide to the form and ntent of Kathakaḷi dance-drama, one of the major ditional classical theatre forms of India. It is designed marily for the interested layman but contains considerable chnical data and information not previously found in the) few publications on Kathakaḷi dance-drama that have peared in the past. Certainly far more can be said of the of Kathakaḷi. The dramatic literature, or āṭṭakatha, fully nslated with traditional interpolations alone could fill veral volumes. The continuity is a series of descriptive says integrated with photographic images; speaking gether, these give as direct an introduction to Kathakaḷi as possible within the given limitations.

explanation of the transliteration scheme and basic onunciation of Malayalam and Sanskrit terms used is ovided. A selected glossary of terms at the back of the book ould prove useful.

e publication coincides with the present 1970 world tour the celebrated Kerala Kalamandalam Kathakaḷi Troupe m the Kerala State academy of theatre art in India. The pearance of the Kalamandalam Kathakaḷi players in the ited States is through the auspices of the American Society Eastern Arts, San Francisco. We wish to express our preciation of the sustained interest and enthusiasm of the esident of the American Society for Eastern Arts, Samuel ripps, for bringing to the stages of the United States one India's greatest theatre arts.

ecial thanks and acknowledgment are due to the faculty d staff of Kerala Kalamandalam, particularly to M. K. Raja mpuran, retired Secretary of Kerala Kalamandalam, zhenkata Kunjan Nayar Āśān, T. T. Ramankutti Nayar Āśān, Padmanabhan Nayar Āśān, P. V. Govinda Warrier Āśān, Vasudevan Nambudrippad, and M. P. Sankaran Nambudri. any technical points were clarified through long and eresting discussions with these gentlemen, and with P. S. Menon, whose publications on Kathakaḷi (in alayalam) are invaluable, and with C. Balakrishnan rup whose father, Mahakavi Vallathol Narayana Menon, founded Kalamandalam some forty years ago. Our thanks go also to the present Chairman of the Executive Committee of Kalamandalam, Mr. M. K. K. Nair, and to the secretary of Kalamandalam, Mr. Sivasankara Pillai.

Many happy if strenuous hours spent in watching Kerala's famous all-night performances have also added considerably to our knowledge and appreciation of the art on both sides of the curtain.

We should here like to record our appreciation of the exacting work put forth by Sara Stalder and Eve Louie, who helped prepare the final text for the printers. Photographs other than those by Mrs. Steward appearing among the illustrations are by Kerala Kalamandalam, Graeme Vanderstoel, Betty Rae Eisenstein, or the authors. Especially we appreciate the imaginative and sensitive treatment of the book design and illustrations by Jan Steward.

The Authors.
University of Pennsylvania,
Philadelphia. May, 1970

PRONUNCIATION AND DIACRITICAL MARKS

The transliteration of any Indian language into English always presents some problems. Since the English alphabet has fewer letters, a system of using diacritical marks is necessary if the spelling is to be accurate. There is also the ever present problem of pronunciation.

The vowels are comparatively simple. The following table is taken from Gundert's Malayalam and English Dictionary (Kottayam: Sahitya Pravarthaka C. S. Ltd., 2nd ed., 1962, p. 21):

a as a in about	ū as u in rule	o as o in collect
ā as a in far	e as ea in head	ō as o in vote
i as i in pin	ē as ea in swear	au as ou in house
ī as i in police	ai as ei in height	am as um in fulcrum
u as u in full		

In Malayalam words a final u is usually slighted in pronunciation and almost omitted.

As for the consonants, c in a transliterated Malayalam or Sanskrit word is pronounced as ch in chapter. This may seem unnecessarily abstruse, but most consonants in Indian languages have an aspirated form and if ch is used for the unaspirated form, there is every likelihood of eventually finding a word with "chchh" occurring in it, which is perhaps even more abstruse. Aspirated t (th) is pronounced as in pothole rather than as in theory; likewise ph is pronounced as in cuphook. Both ṣ and ś may be pronounced as English sh in shape. It will not be important to the general reader to distinguish between other retroflex forms with the dot beneath and the dentals without the dot; using the dental pronunciation for both will serve the purpose.

A peculiarity of Malayalam is that the consonants k, c, ṭ, t, and p, if they are not doubled and occur between two vowels, are pronounced g, j, ḍ, d, and b. It should be mentioned also that ṇṭ and nt are pronounced ṇḍ and nd.

Some other consonants which may not
be readily decipherable:
ñ is pronounced as the ny in canyon
ṅ is pronounced as the first occurrence of ng in singing (Malayalam ങ)
zh is pronounced almost like English r (Malayalam ഴ)
ṟ is a well trilled r (Malayalam റ). When doubled, this is transliterated as ṯṯ since this follows the pronunciation which is like English t.

Diacriticals have been avoided in place names and names of persons except in the case of historical figures.

CONTENTS

1

INTRODUCTION

The State of Kerala lies like a great green staircase on the Southwest Coast of India. It descends to the sea from the granite heights of the cool Western Ghats, beribboned with rivers winding through forests of teak and gardens of spices, through flooded fields of brilliant green rice paddy, through red laterite earth and white sands, through the eddying backwaters, palm fringed lakes and canals, finally to the sparkling Indian Ocean. The country is green, the cool lush green of the southern tropics; coconut palms, spreading mangoes, plumeria and hibiscus are everywhere. As seen from the sea, Kerala is an endless slash of green on the approaching horizon between the dark blue of the water and the limitless blue of the sky. From the air it is a sudden breathtaking checkerboard of glittering flooded fields and feathery green palms. The cities, towns, and villages are virtually obliterated from sight under a protective covering of green.

The pervasive architectural style of the countryside is simple unadorned white plaster walls, palm-thatch or earth-red tile roofs and woven bamboo garden fences. Here and there are the villas and palaces of the old aristocracy; temples, mosques and cathedrals stand among the trees. In the major cities and ports are the crowds, the noise, the towers and offices of administration and production, the activity, the bustle of business, export and import — evidence of the continuous trade with the outside world that comes to Kerala's shores.

From before the dawn of the Christian Era, Imperial Rome traded with Kerala as did Egypt, Arabia, and China in later times. The oldest merchant communities of Christians and Jews in Asia are to be found in Kerala, for many of them a refuge from oppression. For well over a thousand years Kerala has been the home of a large Muslim trading community. The Portuguese, Dutch, Danes, and English were attracted to the shores of fabled Malabar between the 16th and 18th centuries by the promise of wealth from the spice trade. Out of the varied struggle for the gold of pepper, cloves, cardamom, and cinnamon, the political and cultural interchange has ultimately enriched the land and people of Kerala. Minority ethnic groups may speak many languages, but all speak Malayalam, the language of Kerala. And all consider themselves Malayalis belonging to Kerala.

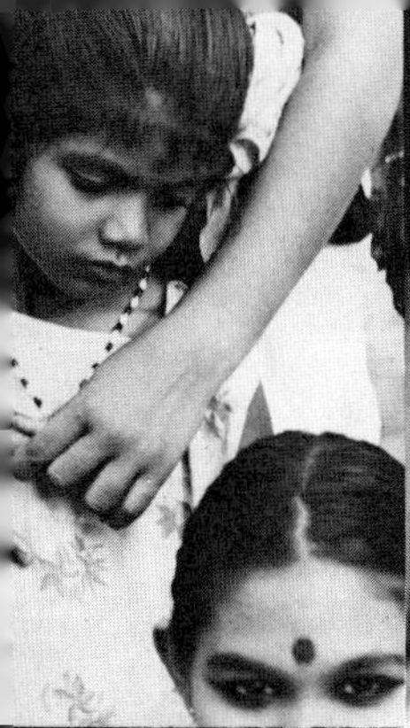

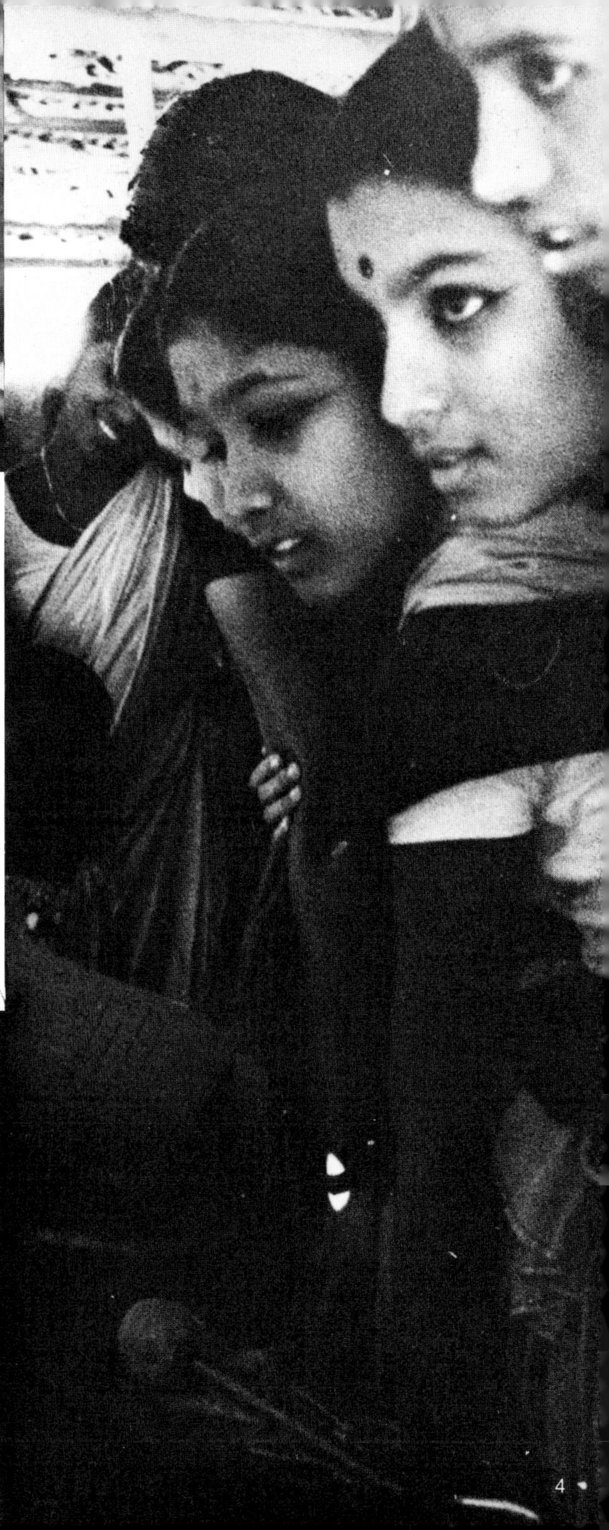

The predominant taste in dress of the Malayali is a plain white; particularly for special occasions, it will be adorned with a bit of black or gold. But there are also the opulent purple and gold shot silks, brilliant pinks, and emerald greens worn by Muslim ladies, and the orange, black, royal blues and reds of the Tamil and Kanarese immigrants. Businessmen in the large cities and factory centers wear the inevitable international tropical uniform of white suit and black tie, or more simply white slacks and sport shirt. Near the sea coast people wear bold black, green, or blue plaids on work days. Everywhere young school girls wear flowers in their hair. Thousands of children crowd the streets and byways on their way to and from school. Continuous moving friezes of people bustle back and forth against an unchanging tropical green. These are but a part of the colors and images, the textures and visual substance of the setting in which we find the art of Kathakaḷi.

Away from the business of the day, in a suburb outside the city or in a village in the interior, toward late afternoon the light grows orange as the sun slowly disappears behind a dark lattice of coconut palms on its way to melt into the sea. This is the beginning of sandhya, the juncture or meeting of day and night. The high contrasts and juxtapositions of color are muted, the hurried, agitated impressions of the day begin to sort themselves out, there is a space in time. The pause is marked by the ritual lighting of lamps, one by one, winking on in the gathering dusk through the trees. The air is st

almost breathless. A tiny bat silently wheels by on the beginning of his nocturnal flight. Then in the early evening very suddenly clearly you may hear the sharp, bell-like drums of the kēḷikkoṭṭu announce that nearby tonight there will be a Kathakaḷi drama performed. There are preparations to be made. Booths for coffee and tea must be provided; there will be vendors of sweets and savories. If it is a festival, an entire temporary bazaar will spring up nearby with novelties of every kind from jasmine flowers and balloons to ribbons and glass bangles.

Throughout the night,

until the cool hours of dawn,

the magic world of

India's ancient epics will live again,

evoked and captured

by the art of Kathakaḷi,

an art which is both ritual

and theatre

and perhaps the best of both,

certainly one of the

genuine timeless treasures

of the Malabar Coast.

THE TRADITION AND THE PREPARATION

Kathakaḷi, India's major traditional dance-drama form from Kerala State, is a synthesis of many arts and periods of development built upon the framework of the Sanskrit tradition in theatre and strongly influenced by the indigenous Dravidian culture of the South. The State of Kerala is famous for its literally hundreds of forms of dance and dance-drama — ritual, folk, and classical. The crowning achievement of these hundreds of years of tradition is Kathakaḷi.

As a drama form, it stands historically in a similar relationship to its predecessor as does Kabuki to the earlier form of Noh drama in Japan. Dating from the end of the 16th century with a written literary form from the 17th century, Kathakaḷi has its roots in much older forms. It is significantly linked to Kūṭiyāṭṭam, the only surviving traditional form for presenting Sanskrit drama extant in India today. Kathakaḷi is the historically later, more popular dramatic form and Kūṭiyāṭṭam the earlier, more rigidly classical. The living theatre tradition of Kūṭiyāṭṭam is at least as old as the 10th century; many scholars maintain its earlier root form to be as early as the 5th to 2nd century A.D. on the basis of a reference to a Cākyār actor in the ancient Tamil story, Śilappadikāram. The Cākyārs indeed are the hereditary actors of Kūṭiyāṭṭam Sanskrit drama today.

Other aspects of antiquity are revealed in the structural continuity of the two traditions. Both Kūṭiyāṭṭam and Kathakaḷi, in staging, techniques, and conventions, are in close agreement with ancient Indian dramatic theory. In the Sanskrit treatises on dramaturgy, especially the Bharata Nāṭyaśāstra,[1] are found a surprising number of specific instances where the present traditions of Kūṭiyāṭṭam and Kathakaḷi are either in agreement with, or show a specific development of, the concepts laid down in those ancient works. A stunning example is the survival into the present of a classical theatre architecture tradition for Kūṭiyāṭṭam in the temples of Kerala which unquestionably demonstrates the theory of the śilpa śāstras on theatre construction. A later medieval text, the Hastalakṣaṇadīpika,[2] is the acknowledged handbook on mudrā, or gesture, for both Kūṭiyāṭṭam and Kathakaḷi.

In its present form the rich and bizarre variety of Kathakaḷi makeup, costuming, and ornaments seems to draw inspiration from Kerala's traditional painting and sculpture of the 16th century, a development of still earlier influences from Tamilnad and Mysore from about the 12th century.

Beyond this classical base, there is a second element of abiding vitality. To what extent elements of folk ritual have been absorbed into the classical tradition or elements from the classical mode have been adopted into the folk tradition, remains an unresolved question. It is evident, however, that a powerful ritualistic undertone pervades Kathakaḷi. Scenes of symbolic death or destruction of agents of evil by the Puranic gods and heroes in Kathakaḷi drama closely parallel the folk rituals which form a part of religious festivals. This is further reinforced by evidence of parallels in priestly mudrā and Tantrik ritual concepts. The Tantrik tradition in South India enjoyed great prestige in the historical period contemporary with the emergence of Kathakaḷi as a sacred dance-drama form. The magical symbols of the initial evocation, cycles of progressive action, strength, endurance, perfection in execution, and the final resolution are ritual concepts common to both the tradition of the temple and that of the theatre.

There are two other aspects of extreme importance in the development of Kathakaḷi. One is the tradition of the kaḷari, which is best translated as military gymnasium. The method, discipline, and technique of body movement owe much to what was once the fine practice of arms in the medieval period. The other aspect which one must take into account is that of the tradition in patronage. There is a long history of patrons from the traditional nobility at the head of which stood the hereditary princes, priestly families, and feudal lords of the land, all belonging to a strongly Sanskritized elite. From this group came material support, intimate contact with the temple-based Sanskrit theatre, and the continuity of a dramatic literary tradition, already much identified with epic themes. From the same aristocracy came the leading authors of āṭṭakatha, the plays themselves which form the base of the repertoire of Kathakaḷi even today. While Kathakaḷi now has a broader, more popular, patronage, it is still the descendants of the families of the traditional patrons who form the inner core of the real aficionados of this very special art form.

ery much like the special world of Tauromaquia, from which e borrow the term aficionado, the world of Kathakaḷi has its rvent devotees, a complex of terminologies and rituals, nd exacting standards of discrimination and appreciation. ne extremely devoted, the Kathakaḷi bhrāntan or those hom "Kathakaḷi madness" has touched, will serenely sit rough five- to nine-hour performances for several days in ıccession. After the marathon of an all-night performance, ey will discuss point by point the actors' interpretations nd technique of the previous night until high noon of the llowing day — only then bestirring themselves for a freshing bath and a quick something at the teashop before, y bus, train, or a friend's overcrowded car, pushing on to the ext night's performance. One must be very durable — the aying season lasts for months until again the cycle of the onsoon returns.

The time of the monsoon scarcely dampens the ardor of the one really mad for Kathakaḷi, for he will invariably be found, if he is especially privileged, watching the intensive training which takes place in the cool months of the rainy season. There in flickering lamplight long before dawn the gymnastics and physical exercise which develop incredible stamina and flexibility take place in daily non-stop cycles from 3 A.M. to 7 A.M. A very special feature of this phase of the training is the oil massage performed by the masters of the Kathakaḷi actor's art, who bear the title Āśān. The final massage is accomplished with the feet, used as hands, and the added weight of the teacher, to create the requisite hyper-flexibility and 180° turn-out perfection demanded by this incredibly exacting theatre tradition. This phase of the training is completed by a chilling plunge in the nearby river, the confirmation of a Spartan military heritage.

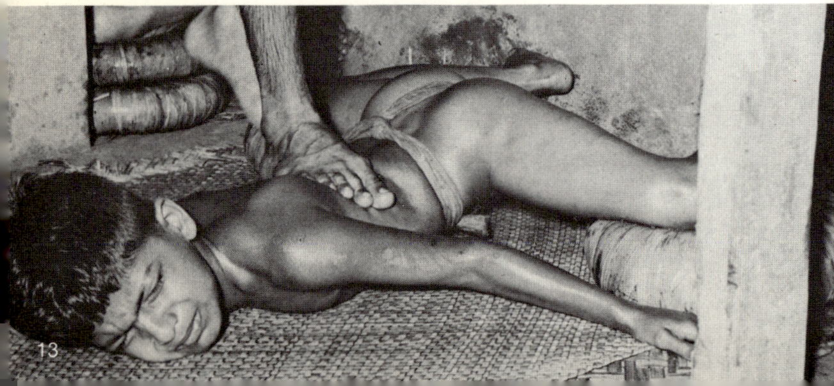

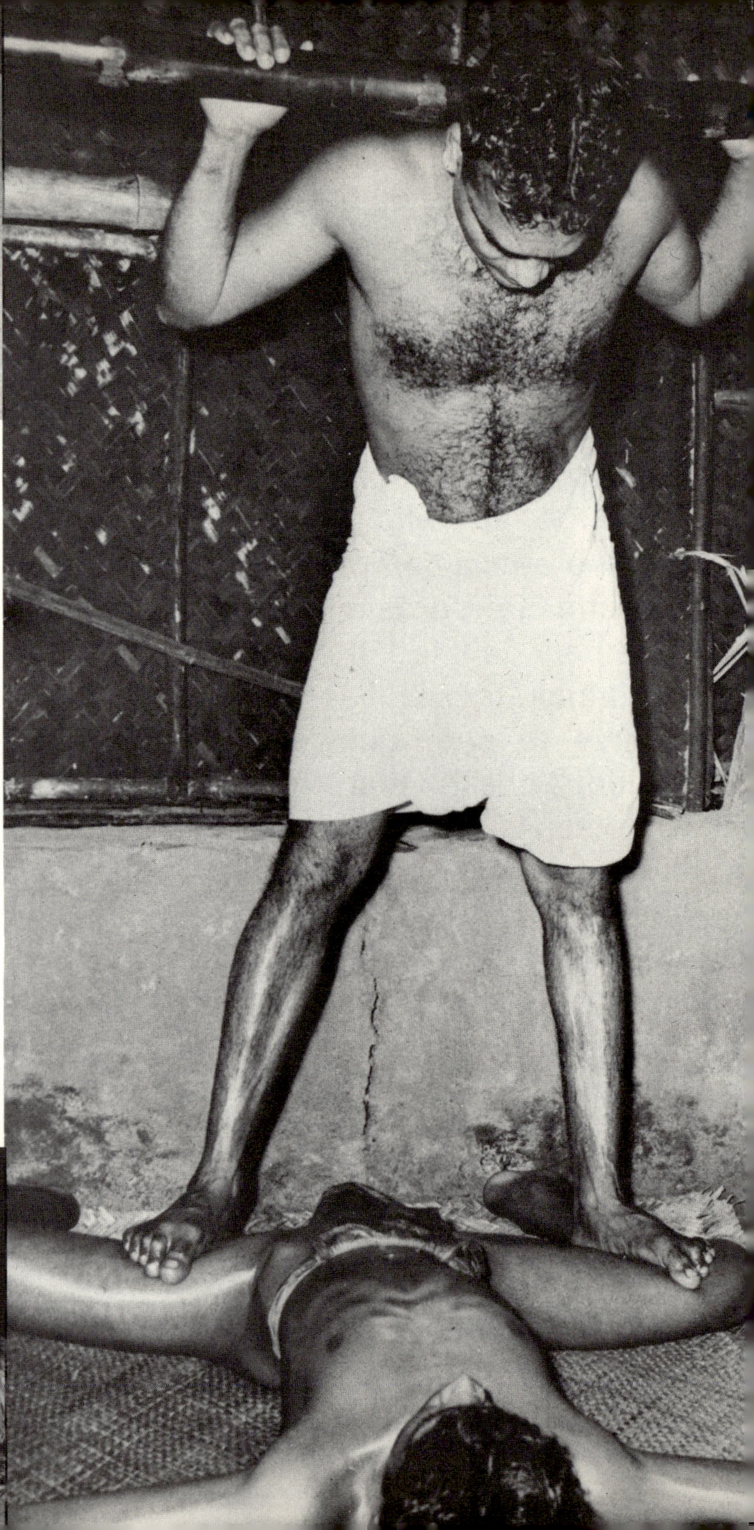

The military heritage of Kerala is a firm part of the physical and technical foundation of Kathakaḷi. As mentioned elsewhere, the pattern of persistence, continuity, and completion of the cycle of events is a strong psychological thread in the Kerala tradition. When these elements are applied to the training of young Kathakaḷi actors-to-be, beginning from the age of twelve, continuing through a classic regime of eight to twelve years, they produce a discipline and technical command that is legendary. The elements of discipline are not only those identifiable with the military tradition of the past, but those that still form a part of the discipline of the old traditional extended family unit, the taṟavāṭu. The term taṟavāṭiṭṭam is difficult to define. In broad terms it means a decorum and manner that speak eloquently of a fine family tradition and upbringing, of unquestionable honesty and loyalty, respect, pride and belief in one's tradition. These qualities are emphasized in the training of Kathakaḷi actors, and combined with the relentless physical training characteristic of the old military tradition, produce the finest of artists. From among the best there will emerge in each generation those few destined for greatness. The qualities sought for in a student are several; it is rare to find a perfect balance of that special type of face and features, that physical resilience and determination, and the ability to retain the staggering body of literary and technical material that must be committed to memory. And then the actor must make it all come alive, ultimately transcending the ritual of formal technique into the ritual of a great living art form which is often a kind of very personal religion.

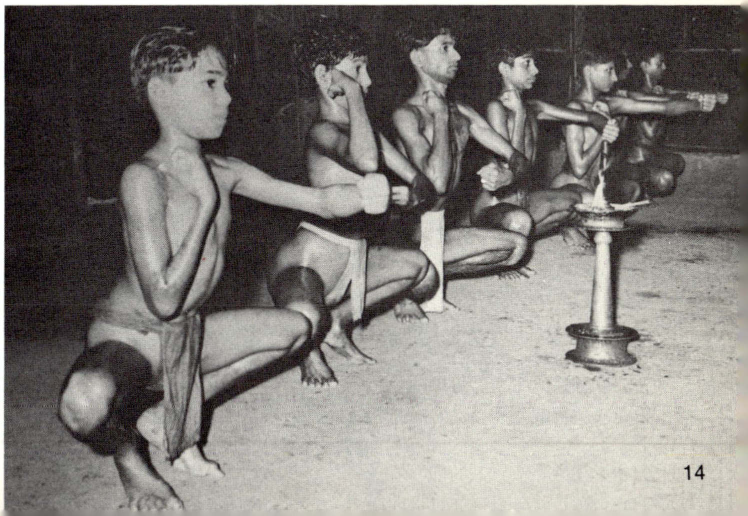

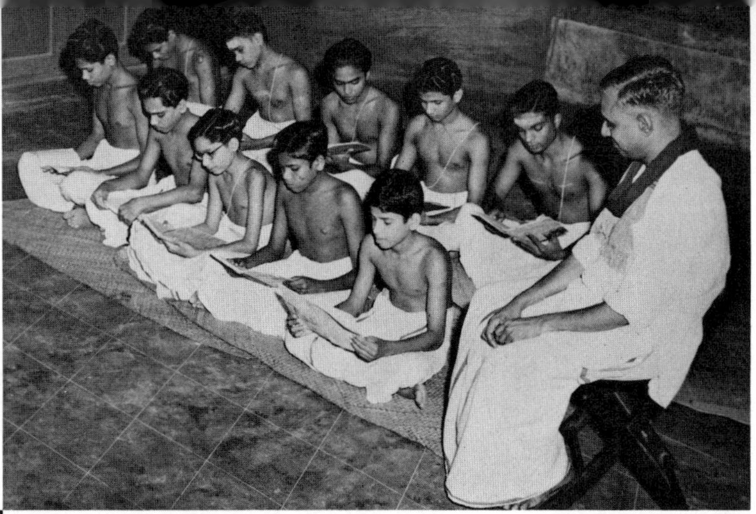

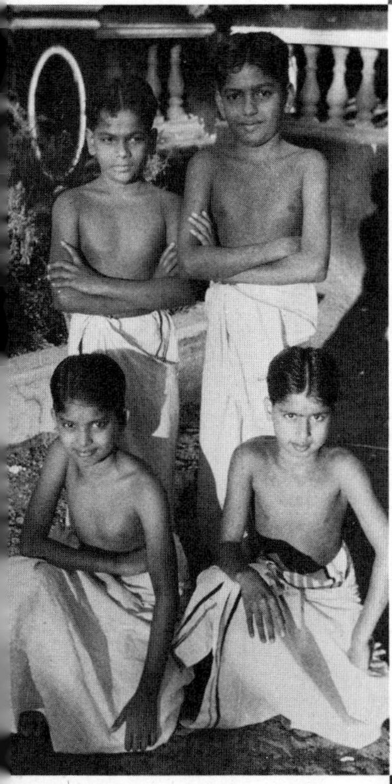

By 8:30 colliyāṭṭam, the major rehearsal of repertoire for the day, begins and continues until noon. A two-hour class period of mudrā and abhinaya (gesture and acting) in the evening, just after the hour of bhajanam or prayer singing, culminates a day in a student's life in the months of June, July, and August. The prescribed cycle of oil massage and intense early morning regimen having been completed, the training continues from September to March on a less rigorous schedule; during that time the first class of the day begins at 8 A.M. rather than 3 A.M. Throughout the training period regular academic subjects are taught: Malayalam and Sanskrit literature, history, mathematics, etc.

The training of Kathakaḷi musicians is accomplished on a similar schedule. The long hours of work, meticulous attention to detail, the building of stamina, the committing to memory of an enormous repertoire, the eventual emergence of individual artistry in which technique becomes a tool rather than an end — the development of the Kathakaḷi musician is in every way comparable to that of the actor.

March, April, and May are the months of the dry hot season in most of India. In South India these are the months of most intense performance in which the practical experience of acting night after night takes precedence over the intense technical training. The experience of the actor — and the musician — is continuous, only the emphasis varies.

It is in the aṇiyar̲a or dressing room that much still is to be learned and savored by the aficionado. It is here that the final ritual of preparation for the actual performance takes place. In the most traditional setting, particularly in the precincts of a temple, the makeup and dressing take place in a room nearest the stage area. The ideal traditional stage is prepared out of doors on a raised plinth of earth, covered with a temporary pavilion open on all sides, the audience seated on mats surrounding the stage on three sides with its greatest concentration centered immediately before the stage. In the dressing room preparations for a performance have begun three to four hours in advance of the first curtain. Young students and dressers under the direction of the senior makeup artist, who is often the master costumer as well, begin the preparation of the pigments for the elaborate makeup and lay out the parts of the costumes, gilded and jewelled ornaments, and crowns in their time-honored prescribed order. The senior actors whose roles for that evening will require elaborate and time-consuming detail appear first and begin. The whole process down to the preparation of the smallest role is arranged in time sequence to avoid confusion or last-minute panic in making entrance cues.

The atmosphere of the dressing room is subdued, intent, concentrated. The elaborate transformation of professional actor into epic character is taking place before one's eyes. Bit by bit the individual personality is obliterated by elaborate painted patterns and finally after an hour or more under the hands of the master artist, who applies the fragile white cuṭṭi, he is still further transformed. The elaborate facial makeup is done; the actor rises to be dressed by trained assistants. Again he sits and carefully places inside the lower lid of each eye a cuṇṭappūvu seed. Within minutes his eyes are a brilliant inflamed rose red. Then, balancing a mirror at a precise angle between the two upturned soles of his feet, he begins the final elaborate tying of the remainder of the "one hundred knots." At this time the under turban cushioning the considerable weight of the carved, gilded and jewelled wooden crown is tied in place; the large lower ear ornaments, kuṇḍala, are attached; then the magnificent kēśabhāra kirīṭam, the jewelled nimbate crown, is settled in place and secured by the tying of the cuṭṭi tuṇi, cevippūvu, and neṯṯi bandham in quick succession — and finally the cāmaram or long black wig is tied in place. The last act of the actor's dressing is to redden his palms with a rose tinted powder and then with careful precision one by one place the sparkling long silver talons on each of the fingers of his left hand. Facing a lighted lamp the actor pauses in meditation, then in respect touching the feet and receiving the blessing of the senior actors present, he leaves for the stage — girded like some fantastic royal gladiator for the test of his craft.

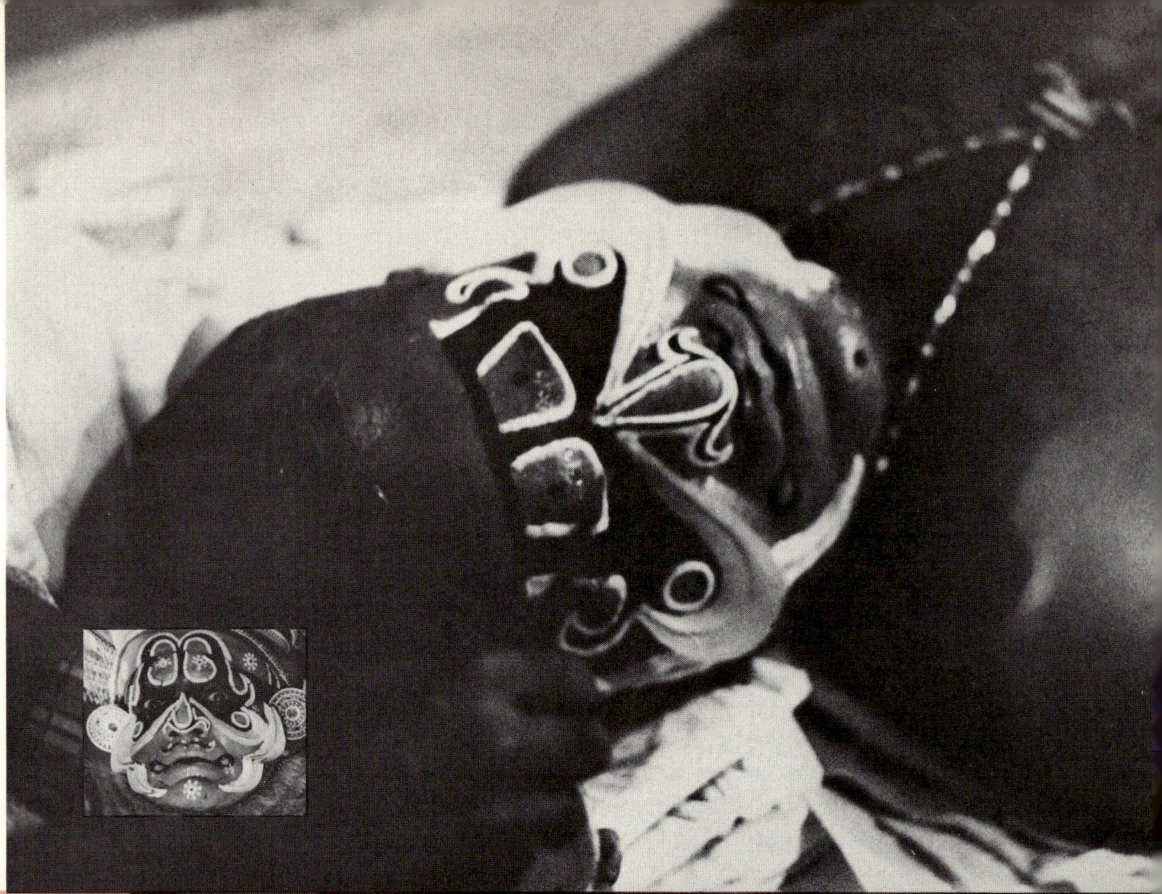

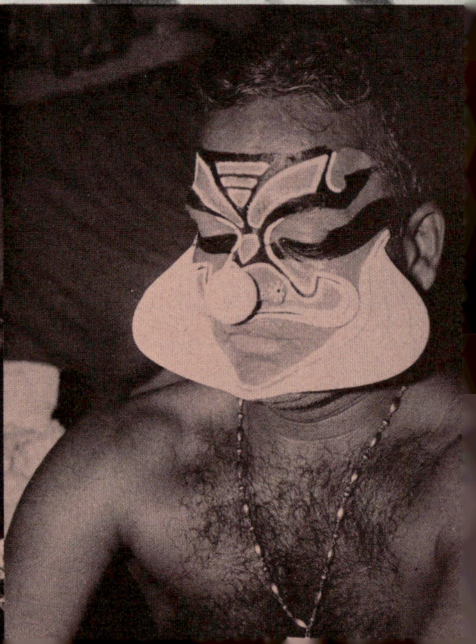

THE COSTUME AND MAKEUP

One of the mystifying and bizarre features of the Kathakaḷi performance to those who see it for the first time, is the apparent similarity of many characters in dress and makeup. They seem strangely abstract creatures with bright green or golden or striped red, white and black faces, with black painted wings for eyes and, on some, even false white fangs and a matte white "mushroom" for a nose. The makeup of Kathakaḷi is indeed mystifying to the uninitiated. There is no particular preoccupation with realism, though many characters, especially women and sages and servants, are more nearly naturalistic in conception. The great characters of Kathakaḷi, the demons and heroes of ancient epic literature, are the most abstract. All characters fall into the basic stylistic categories known as pacca, katti, tāṭi, kari, tēppu, and minukku. Know them and their types and you will know the characters and their psychological temperaments in the drama. There are numerous variations to be sure, but a classic typology governs all.

The Pacca. These are the heroic, kingly, and divine types, those who wear the kēśabhāra kirīṭam, the jewelled crown. subcategory is called muṭi, those who wear a sparkling vase-shaped silver crown topped with a circlet fringe of peacock feather tips. To this latter category belong the incarnations of the God Viṣṇu, such as Rāma or Kṛiṣṇa. Bot of these categories are distinguished by and have in comm a glittering bright green painted face with velvet black brov and eyes and a red-orange matte mouth. On the forehead is a nāmam, a stylized sacred mark of Viṣṇu. They wear also the characteristic basic cuṭṭi, the elaborate white paste and paper frame, extending from the cheek bones from both sides of the jaw, descending in a curve to join at the apex of the chin.

Similar to the pacca in makeup pattern and costume is the rare division called pazhuppu. Where the pacca makeup ba is green, the pazhuppu is a light orange-gold. The basic colors of the costume are blue and red; the ornaments and crown (kirīṭam) are the same. Characters such as Brahmā, Śiva, and Balabhadra appear in this special makeup.

The Katti. This is a class of personality type generally demonic in nature but with some noble characteristics. Examples of this type are Duryodhana and the demon King Rāvaṇa, ill-starred villains ultimately defeated by the uncontrollable desire and egotism. Their faces are basica the green of the pacca with the same basic painting of the eyes and a similar cuṭṭi. A red and white stylized mustach extends from cheek to cheek. The red and white pattern i carried up over the nose, between the eyes, and spreads upon the forehead in a knife-shaped design over each eyebrow. From this pattern comes the name katti which means "knife." A white knob is attached to the nose as a abstract touch. This character type usually wears the ide costume and crown of the royal heroic pacca type, hence the importance of understanding the convention and the distinctions of character typology.

The Tāṭi. The term tāṭi means "bearded." There are three types in this class. One is the "red beard" or cukannattāṭi, the demonic, unregenerate evil anti-hero. This sub-class h variations, such as the characters of Vāli (also called Bāli) and Sugrīva who are on the contrary good but egocentric belong to the lesser world of man-animals. The classic cukannattāṭi is readily recognized not only by his red bear but by his towering, oversized crown. His upper face is bla the lower jaw red, his huge white mustache curves up to h ears, and he has an oversized doorknob-like false nose. H whole character is gross, exaggerated, crude, menacing, and sometimes slightly comical.

'he second sub-division within this class is the veḷḷattāṭi or "white beard." The principal veḷḷattāṭi is Hanumān, the monkey devotee of Rāma. He has conventionalized simian features, red, black and white, and is easily identified by his furry white acket and wide-brimmed headdress with courses of sparkling pendants and a white and silver finial. The veḷḷattāṭi is kind, :apricious, wise, devoted, but ferocious when enraged.

last sub-division of this group is the "black beard" or karuttatāṭi, a demonic type, identical with the red beard except for r and minor variant details.

The Kari is the black type for demonesses such as Śūrpaṇakhā in the Rāmāyaṇa. When a lalita character changes back to her horrific form this is the costume designated. The basic colors are black, red, and white. A bucket-shaped headdress, wider at the top, in black, white, silver, and fringed with peacock feathers, is a distinctive feature of the costume. Comic false breasts and false fangs are worn and a pathetic "feminine" touch is a red and white "apron." Kaṭuttatāṭi is a related male costume for hunters such as Kāṭṭāḷan, the disguise of Śiva in the story of "Kirātam." The same headdress is worn as for the kari character. The lower garment is blue or black and the rest of the details are black and red. This character wears a black beard and a white "daisy" on the end of his nose. Both the kari and kaṭuttattāṭi are meant to be comical, satirical, and grotesque.

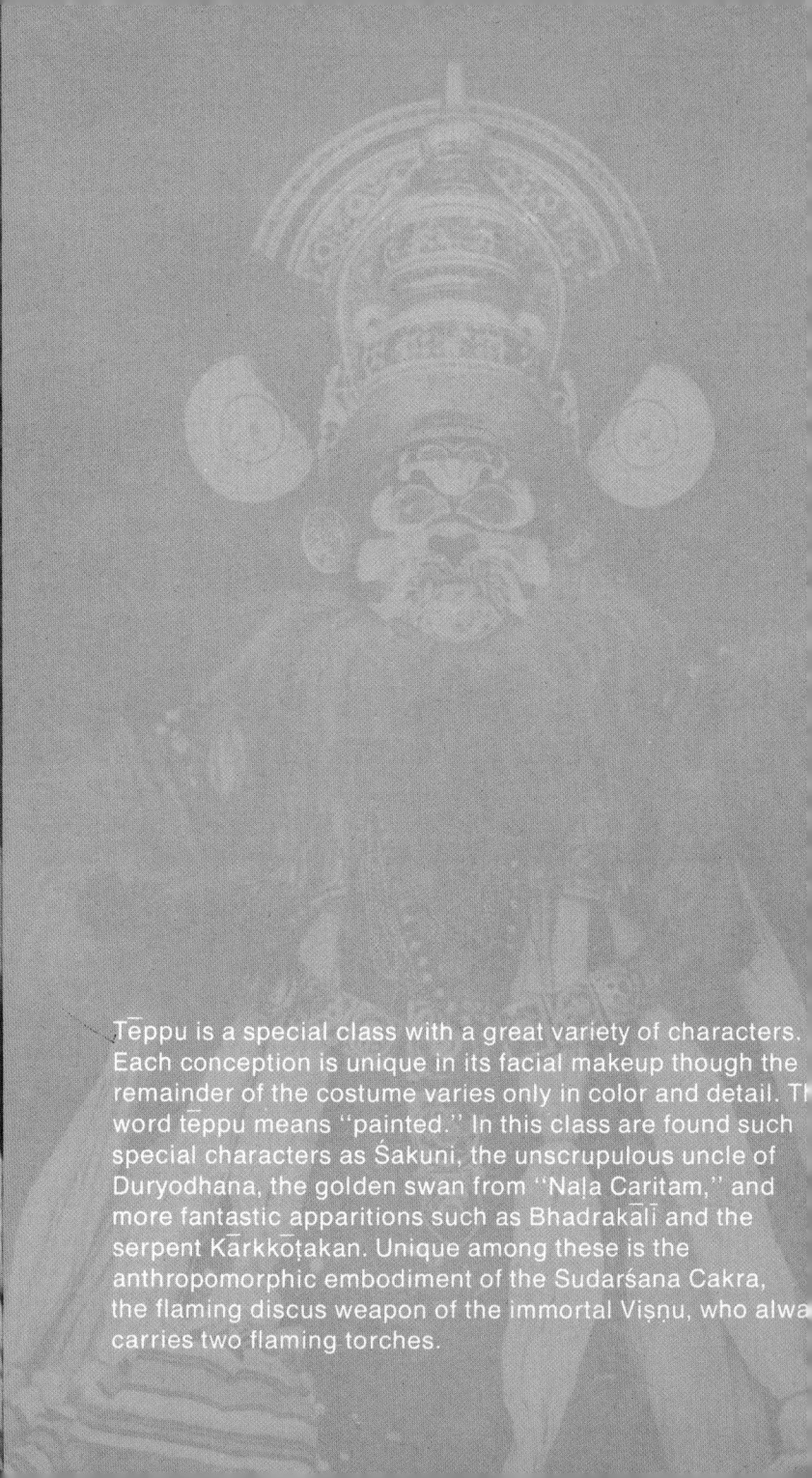

Teppu is a special class with a great variety of characters. Each conception is unique in its facial makeup though the remainder of the costume varies only in color and detail. T word teppu means "painted." In this class are found such special characters as Śakuni, the unscrupulous uncle of Duryodhana, the golden swan from "Naḷa Caritam," and more fantastic apparitions such as Bhadrakālī and the serpent Kārkkōṭakan. Unique among these is the anthropomorphic embodiment of the Sudarśana Cakra, the flaming discus weapon of the immortal Viṣṇu, who alwa carries two flaming torches.

Minukku, the "shining" type, includes the more realistic makeup types, such as female characters, whether servants, handmaidens, heroines, or lalitas. The last are demonesses transformed for the time into magically beautiful women, women who are "too beautiful" and therefore suspicious. Included in this group also are sages, kindly or choleric, and Brāhmaṇas, royal pages, messengers, and charioteers. The last three wear silver bordered red turbans and smart black mustaches. All these characters have less stylized makeup on a foundation of golden matte base with a dusting of transparent, glittering, mica. Female characters are further distinguished with brilliant headscarves, special ornaments, jewelled nose rings, and with their hair knotted on the left side. Sages wear beards and have their hair knotted on top of their heads and carry loops of holy beads.

in the medieval art tradition carved and painted in tapestry-like profusion in the major temples in every part of Kerala. They are all visual characterizations well known to the people from childhood.

Underlying all these classifications are the permutations of the psychological qualities embodied in the quasi-scientific philosophical system of the guṇas, the ancient triple division of all reality into sattva or balanced pure-divine; rajas, active, dynamic, irascible; and tamas, inert, impure, base.

Besides the specific color reference to the greater scheme of characterization, identification, and psychological amplification, there is the additional aspect of alaṅkāra, or ornamentation simply for the sake of beautification and opulence, which is another axiom of Indian art generally. The costumes are all ultimately heightened stylizations of jewelry and costume of antiquity as developed from medieval Kerala motifs. The preoccupation with details of embellishment perhaps reaches its pinnacle with the addition of the vegetable seed called cuṇṭappūvu which inflames the whites of the eyes in a range of color from rose for heroes and heroines in love, to sparkling ruby red for the roles of fabulous demons.

THE PRELIMINARIES

The preliminaries have already begun while the actors w will appear first were completing their wardrobe. The opening items preceding the beginning of a Kathakaḷi dance-drama are a traditional series of compositions of virtuoso drumming, vocal music, and dance. There is a s percussion interlude at the very beginning. In the past th was followed by Tōṭayam, a pure dance composition. Tōṭayam was not meant to be seen by the audience and performed while the curtain or tiraśśīla was being held. I today virtually disappeared from popular performance ar is seen only rarely, although it is savored by the orthodo "Kathakaḷi mad" and is still meticulously learned and practiced by students. It is an ideal "training piece" sinc uses many different tālas or rhythms and contains much the choreographic range of the pure dance technique of Kathakaḷi.

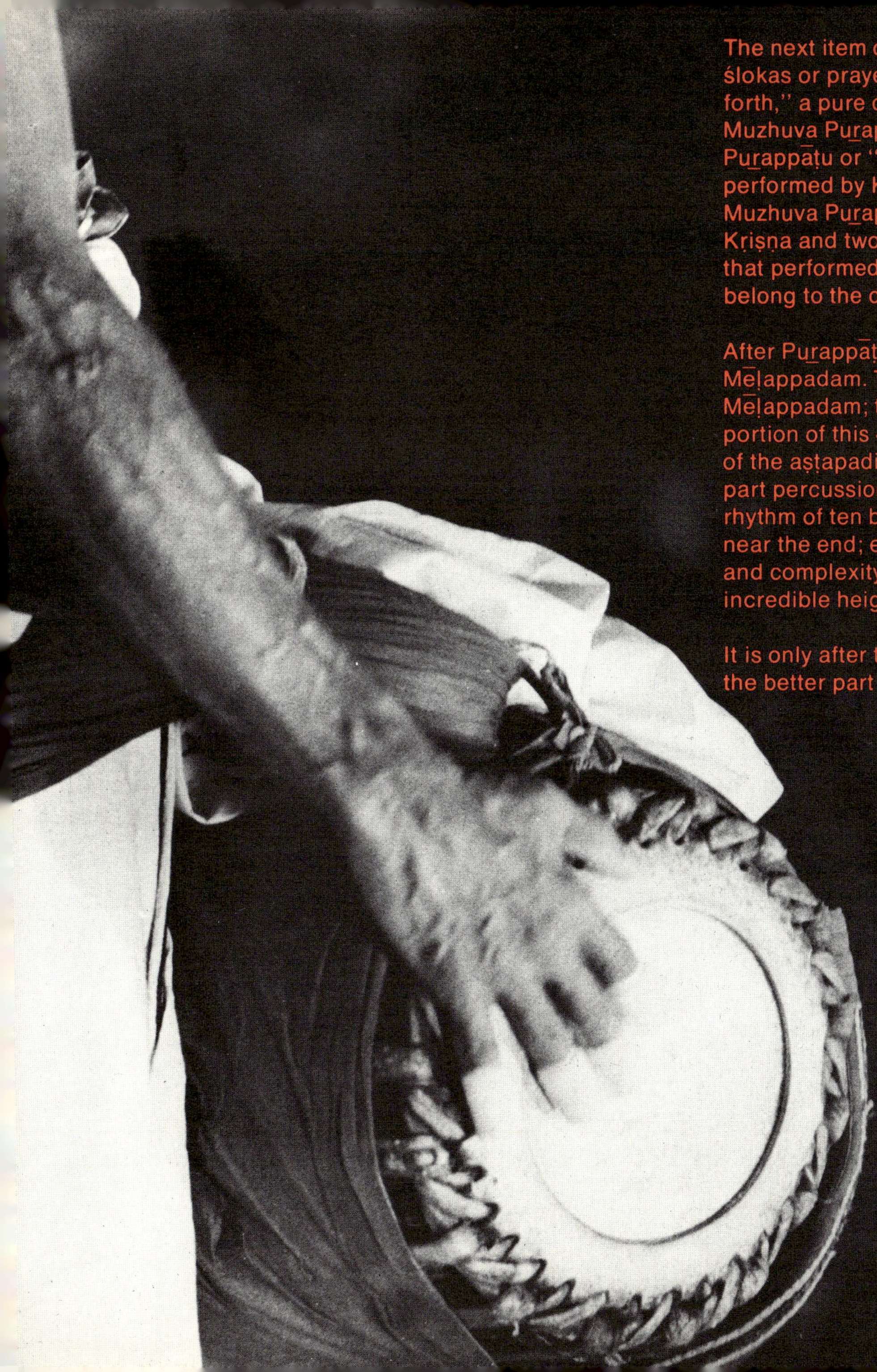

The next item of the preliminaries is the singing of vandana ślokas or prayers. This is followed by Puṟappāṭu or "going forth," a pure dance composition which has two varieties, Muzhuva Puṟappāṭu or "full Puṟappāṭu" and Pakuti Puṟappāṭu or "half Puṟappāṭu." The latter variety is performed by Kṛṣṇa and his brother Balabhadra. The other, Muzhuva Puṟappāṭu, is often performed by two Kṛṣṇas or Kṛṣṇa and two consorts. The ideal Muzhuva Puṟappāṭu is that performed by the main characters of heroic nature who belong to the drama to follow.

After Puṟappāṭu will come the elaborate composition called Mēḷappadam. There is no dancing or acting during Mēḷappadam; the musicians hold the stage. The vocal portion of this 45-minute composition is the singing of one of the aṣṭapadis from Jayadeva's Gīta Govinda; in the last part percussion takes precedence. The Mēḷappadam is in a rhythm of ten beats, changing to a rhythm of sixteen beats near the end; each drummer takes solos, increasing in speed and complexity. Each one, trying to surpass the other, reaches incredible heights of virtuosity and improvisation.

It is only after these elaborate preliminaries, which can take the better part of two hours, that the drama proper begins.

ĀṬṬAKATHA

The poetic text for a Kathakaḷi dance-drama is called āṭṭakatha; it is written especially for Kathakaḷi and is usually in Maṇipravāḷam, a heavily Sanskritized, literary form of Malayalam. The principal literary sources of the plots may be found in the perennial epics of India, the Mahābhārata and the Rāmāyaṇa, and in the Bhāgavata Purāṇa. Some thirty plays are in the current performing repertoire, but the total literature consists of more than one hundred plays.

The first Kathakaḷi plays written were the so-called Rāmanāṭṭam stories, based on the Rāmāyaṇa. They were written by the Rāja of Koṭṭārakkara; there is some doubt as to which Rāja of Koṭṭārakkara was the author, but most authorities in Kerala believe these plays were written between 1655 and 1661.[3]

There are in the current repertoire thirteen plays based on the Mahābhārata. A few years ago it became a popular practice in Kerala to stage "Pūrṇa Bhārata" or "full Mahābhārata." This consists of selected scenes from the plays on Mahābhārata stories, arranged in sequence to make one connected story. The version of the Mahābhārata given here in synopsis form is only a part of the "Pūrṇa Bhārata" which is usually a nine-hour-long performance. Scenes I, V, and VII are from "Duryodhana Vadham," written by Vayaskara Mūss; scenes II, III, and IV are from "Kīcaka Vadham," written by Irayimman Tambi, early 19th century. Scene VI, Bhagavad Gītā, was written only a few years ago by Mannar Gopalan Nayar.

Since the "Pūrṇa Bhārata" proved to be a success, the "full Rāmāyaṇa" also was staged by selecting episodes from the eight Rāmanāṭṭam stories and arranging them in a continuity. The version of the Rāmāyaṇa given here in synopsis form is still further shortened; like "Pūrṇa Bhārata," the full Rāmāyaṇa as usually staged will be about nine hours in duration.

Some among the āṭṭakathas are considered to be of high quality as literature, particularly "Naḷa Caritam" by Uṇṇāyi Vāryyar, 18th century. The complete "Naḷa Caritam" is given on four successive days; only the "First Day's Story" has been given here in synopsis form. The story is taken from the Nalopākhyāna of the Mahābhārata.

A Rāja of Kōṭṭayam, late 17th century, wrote four famous Kathakaḷi plays, all of them regarded as highly classical and among the most popular in the repertoire even today. "Kalyāṇa Saugandhikam" is one of the four and is one of the first stories learned by young students of Kathakaḷi.

"Kirātam," written by Iraṭṭakkuḷaṅṅara Vāryyar, is not considered to be of very high quality as literature; however, as theatre, it is an exceptionally stageworthy piece, and is among the favorites today in Kerala.

Much shortened versions of the āṭṭakathas are given here; also these are "retold" rather than being given in full translation. Most Kathakaḷi dance-dramas in their full form will be from five to seven hours in length. It is now a popular practice in Kerala to have three shortened dramas in one all-night performance.

41

MAHĀBHĀRATA

Scene 1. The Dice Game and Banishment of the Pāṇḍavas
The Pāṇḍavas and their cousins, the Kauravas, are in rivalry. Duryodhana, the eldest of the hundred and one Kauravas, is determined to eliminate the Pāṇḍavas so that he may take over their kingdom. He arranges for his evil uncle, Śakuni, to challenge Yudhiṣṭhira, the eldest of the Pāṇḍavas, to the royal game of dice; Śakuni is known to load the dice. Yudhiṣṭhira is under aristocratic obligation to accept the challenge and the dice game begins.

Yudhiṣṭhira loses each round and everything he stakes. He loses his wealth, his army, and his kingdom. Then, one by one, he stakes his brothers. Finally, he stakes himself and the wife of the five brothers, Draupadī. He loses again. Thus the Pāṇḍavas become the slaves of Duryodhana who now decides to insult and banish them. Duryodhana orders his brother Duhśāsana to drag Draupadī by her hair before him and disrobe her in open court. Duhśāsana carries out the order but Draupadī prays to Lord Kṛiṣṇa; her prayer is answered and after all attempts to disrobe her she remains clothed. The Pāṇḍavas are now slaves without right of protest and watch helplessly; they take a silent vow to avenge Draupadī.

Duhśāsana falls exhausted. In her extreme distress Draupadī curses the Kauravas saying that they will all be killed by her Pāṇḍava husbands. For Duhśāsana the disrober she has a special curse: Bhīma will rip him open and bathe her hair in his blood. Until this takes place Draupadī will not bind up her hair.

Duryodhana banishes the Pāṇḍavas to the forest for twelve years. At the end of the twelve years the Pāṇḍavas are to spend a further year in disguise. If discovered during their year of disguise the Pāṇḍavas must return to the forest for another twelve years, a year in disguise, and so on . . .

(Twelve years have passed and the Pāṇḍavas now live disguised in the kingdom of Virāṭa. Bhīma serves as a cook in the palace kitchen and goes by the name Ballava (called Valalan in Kerala). Draupadī has assumed the name Mālinī and acts as a servant to the queen. The queen's brother, Kīcaka, desires Mālinī and makes advances which are rejected. Vain and unscrupulous, Kīcaka considers himself attractive to all women and will not rest until his desires are fulfilled. Kīcaka confides in his sister and enlists her aid in the affair; together they devise a plan to trap Mālinī. The queen asks Mālinī to take a jug of wine to Kīcaka. Mālinī pleads with the queen to spare her this ordeal but the queen persists and Mālinī reluctantly proceeds to Kīcaka.)

Scene II. Kīcaka and Mālinī
Mālinī enters Kīcaka's house and finds him maddened with lust and wine. He pursues her and is rebuffed. Kīcaka resorts to violence and strikes Mālinī who finally manages to escape.

Scene III. Ballava and Mālinī
Mālinī runs to her husband Ballava and recounts the humiliation she has suffered at the hands of Kīcaka. Ballava, overwhelmed with pity and love, consoles Mālinī and promises to kill Kīcaka. It is decided that Kīcaka should be lured to a secluded part of the palace dancing hall at night in the expectation of finding Mālinī alone.

Scene IV. Kīcaka and Ballava
Kīcaka is overjoyed at the prospect of meeting Mālinī alone at night. He goes to the dancing hall and, in the dim light, finds someone lying there. Ballava leaps at Kīcaka, hurls him to the ground, and strangles him.

Scene V. The Negotiations

(The Pāṇḍavas have completed their thirteen-year term of exile and return to claim a rightful share of the kingdom from their cousins. Yudhiṣṭhira, wishing to avoid war, requests Lord Kṛiṣṇa to negotiate a settlement with Duryodhana. Yudhiṣṭhira is prepared to compromise and, if necessary, accept one house for all the Pāṇḍavas.)

Duryodhana, knowing that Kṛiṣṇa will soon arrive to try to negotiate a settlement, warns the members of his court that anyone who shows respect to Kṛiṣṇa will be punished. Nevertheless, in defiance of this warning, as Kṛiṣṇa appears they all rise to do him honour.

Kṛiṣṇa attempts to negotiate a settlement and first asks for half the kingdom; Duryodhana contemptuously refuses. Kṛiṣṇa reduces the demand to five villages, then to five houses and finally to just one house, but Duryodhana refuses all demands and swears that he will not give the Pāṇḍavas even a pinpoint of land. No settlement being possible, Kṛiṣṇa provokes Duryodhana by argument: Duryodhana becomes angry and orders Kṛiṣṇa to be taken captive. Lord Kṛiṣṇa assumes his cosmic form (viśva rūpa); some of the courtiers, devout and honest men, reverentially worship him, but Duryodhana and his wicked brothers are dazzled and blinded by the sight and fall unconscious to the ground. Kṛiṣṇa disappears to return to the Pāṇḍavas and report the failure of his peace mission.

Scene VI. Bhagavad Gītā

The war is on and the magnificent armies of the Pāṇḍavas
and Kauravas are arrayed against each other on the
battlefield of Kurukṣetra. Arjuna is the Commander-in-Ch
of the Pāṇḍavas; Kṛiṣṇa is acting as his charioteer. Stand
in his chariot, Arjuna looks at the army arrayed against hi
He beholds his teachers, his uncles, his grandfather — al
facing him in battle. Distressed by the thought of warring
his relatives, the valiant Arjuna asks Kṛiṣṇa what victory i
worth if it is achieved over the dead bodies of friends,
relatives, and elders. Arjuna throws away his weapons ar
sits despondently at Kṛiṣṇa's feet.

Kṛiṣṇa is surprised at Arjuna's behaviour. This is a battle
which must be fought — not for gaining personal ends, b
for the establishment of righteousness in the world. Lord
Kṛiṣṇa reveals to Arjuna the true concept of Hindu dharm
or divine order (the discourse known to us as the Bhagav
Gītā). Lord Kṛiṣṇa then assumes his cosmic form and Arj
realizes the truth of the precepts which Kṛiṣṇa has expoun
No longer weak or despondent, Arjuna enters the battle v
courage and determination.

Scene VII. Kurukṣetra

Bhīma and Duhśāsana meet on the field of battle. Bhīma, remembering the insults and humiliation heaped upon Draupadī by the infamous Duhśāsana, is in a frenzy of rage and has assumed the form of a fierce man-lion. After a furious battle, Duhśāsana is defeated and Bhīma rips open his belly and bathes in his blood. Draupadī enters and Bhīma rushes to her, sprinkles blood on her hair, and binds her hair with the entrails. Thus Draupadī's curse is fulfilled.

Suddenly Lord Kṛiṣṇa appears. At the sight of the divine Kṛiṣṇa, Bhīma repents of the animal frenzy which has driven him to such excesses. He falls at the feet of Lord Kṛiṣṇa who blesses him.

Dhanāśi. The concluding dance sequence. For this story, performed by the actor taking the part of Lord Kṛiṣṇa.

RĀMĀYAṆA

The Rāmāyaṇa is the story of Rāma, eldest son of King Daśaratha of Ayodhyā. Under a vow taken at the instigation of Rāma's stepmother, the king reluctantly banishes Rāma to exile for a period of fourteen years. Accompanied by his wife Sītā and his younger brother, Lakṣmaṇa, Rāma goes to a forest hermitage at Pañcavaṭa.

Rāvaṇa is the mighty demon king of Laṅkā (Ceylon).

His sister Śūrpaṇakhā, roaming through the forest one day, is attracted by the handsome brothers, Rāma and Lakṣmaṇa.

As both of them reject her advances, by way of revenge she threatens to harm Sītā.

Lakṣmaṇa disfigures her and chases her away. Rāvaṇa, learning of this, swears vengeance on the two brothers.

Scene I. Rāvaṇa and Mārīca

Rāvaṇa confers with his uncle, Mārīca, and together they devise a scheme to abduct Sītā in order to wreak vengeance on Rāma.

Scene II. The Forest Hermitage at Pañcavaṭa

One day at the hermitage Sītā notices a young deer among the trees. Thinking that the young animal would make a delightful companion, she attempts to catch it, but fails. She asks Rāma for help. As he goes off in pursuit of the deer, he asks Lakṣmaṇa to stand guard over Sītā. After a short time Lakṣmaṇa and Sītā hear a cry for help; it seems to be Rāma's voice. Sītā, fearing that Rāma is in danger, asks Lakṣmaṇa to go to his aid, but Lakṣmaṇa is unwilling to leave her alone in the hermitage. He attempts to pacify her, telling her that Rāma is quite capable of looking after himself. In her anxiety, Sītā abuses Lakṣmaṇa and orders him to go to the aid of his brother.

After Lakṣmaṇa leaves the scene, a samnyāsin (holy man) appears before Sītā and begs alms.

It is Rāvaṇa in disguise and he soon resumes his true form. Sītā is shocked and terrified, but Rāvaṇa only laughs at her helplessness and forcibly carries her off in his flying chariot (puṣpaka vimāna).

Jaṭāyu, the king of birds and an old friend of Rāma's father, hears the sobbing of Sītā. He comes to her rescue and a battle ensues. Rāvaṇa tricks the bird into revealing its weak point and the battle is soon over. Rāvaṇa chops off Jaṭāyu's wings and leaves with Sītā, taking her to Laṅkā.

(On returning to the hermitage Rāma and Lakṣmaṇa realize that they have been tricked. Rāma could not catch the deer; he shot an arrow at the animal which immediately transformed itself into Mārīca and screamed in the voice which misled Sītā. After killing Mārīca, Rāma meets Lakṣmaṇa and together they return to the hermitage and find

that Sītā has disappeared. In their search for Sītā, the brothers arrive at the spot where Jaṭāyu lies wounded.)

Rāma learns from the dying Jaṭāyu that Sītā's abductor is the demon king Rāvaṇa and is advised to seek the assistance of the monkey prince Sugrīva.

Scene III. The Alliance Between Rāma and Sugrīva
(Vāli and Sugrīva are brothers; Vāli, the elder, is king of the monkeys.

He hates Sugrīva and has taken his wife. Sugrīva lives in hiding, awaiting an opportunity for vengeance.)

Rāma and Lakṣmaṇa meet Sugrīva who produces ornaments discarded deliberately by Sītā as she was carried to Laṅkā.

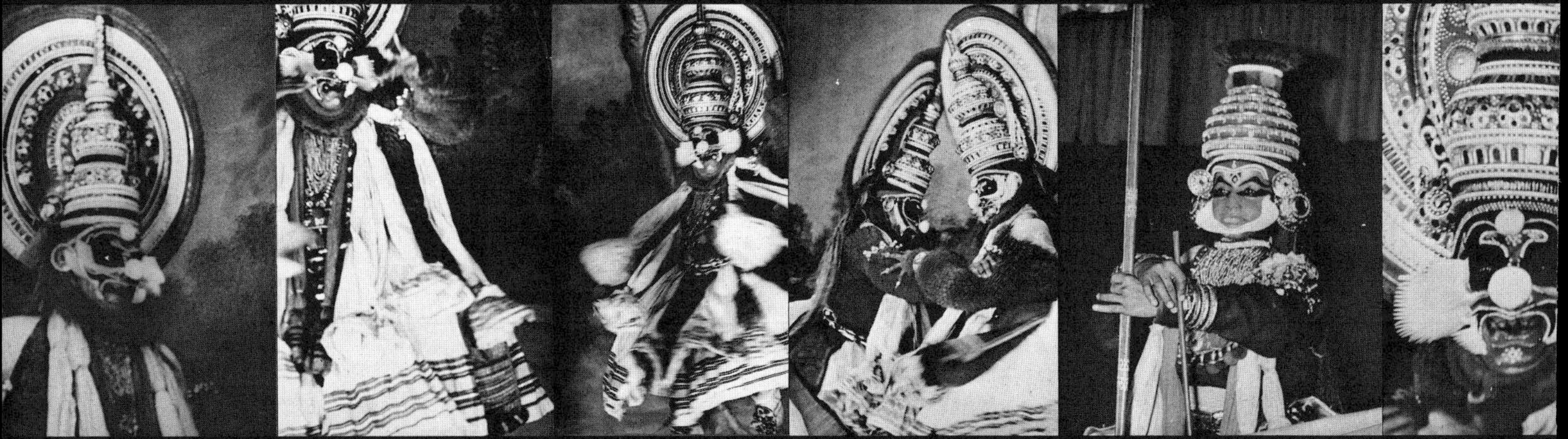

Rāma and Sugrīva enter into an alliance;
Rāma undertakes to help Sugrīva to kill Vāli while Sugrīva promises to place his army at Rāma's disposal to fight Rāvaṇa.

Scene IV. Sugrīva's War Cry
Sugrīva, fortified by his alliance with Rāma, comes out of his hiding place and challenges Vāli to a battle.

Scene V. Death of Vāli

The mighty Vāli cannot believe his ears; Sugrīva whom he has always considered a coward is challenging him. In the fight which follows Sugrīva is no match for Vāli. Rāma, concealed behind a tree, sends an arrow at Vāli. As Vāli falls he realizes it is Rāma's arrow that has struck him down. He reproaches Rāma for shooting the arrow while hidden by the trees. Rāma explains to Vāli that he is being punished for seducing Sugrīva's wife. Vāli's wife, Tārā, and his son, Aṅgada, rush to the scene of the fight. Vāli entrusts his family to Sugrīva's care and dies while invoking the name of God.

Dhanāśi. Performed by Rāma.

The dramatic continuity given above, ending with the deat
of Vāli, is a redaction representing only a part of the full st
the *Rāmāyaṇa.* The subsequent events in which Rāma mee
Hanumān, the divine monkey, and sends him to Laṅkā to seek out Sītā and give her Rāma's signet ring; Hanumān's burning of the city of Laṅkā; the cataclysmic battle, the death of Rāvaṇa and rescue of Sītā; the reunion and the coronation of Rāma at the city of Ayodhyā, are either performed as part of the nine-hour-long "Pūrṇa Rāmāyaṇa
or more usually as separate all-night plays.

NAḶA CARITAM, FIRST DAY'S STORY

a, King of Niṣadha, and Princess Damayantī, daughter ng Bhīma of Kuṇḍina, though they had never met, fell ve through having heard of the beauty and mplishments of each other. Both nursed their love etly until they could no longer suffer separation. Yet er knew the mind of the other or how to reach it. How Naḷa was able to deliver his message of love to ayantī and how they were brought together is the theme e story.)

ne I. King Naḷa and Nārada
sage Nārada arrives at the court of King Naḷa and is ved with great honour. In the course of the conversation, da speaks of the qualities of Princess Damayantī and ests that Naḷa alone, who is the foremost among kings, a right to her hand.

e II. King Naḷa in the Palace Garden
king's love for Damayantī becomes an obsession. It fills s waking hours; he cannot sleep and loses all interest in rs of state. In despair one day he seeks refuge in his en. But the humming bees, singing birds and the me-laden breeze only intensify the pangs of love as if were arrows sent by Kāmadeva, the God of love. With ghts like these, he knows no peace.

Scene III. King Naḷa and the Hamsa

Suddenly his eyes fall on a rare sight, a golden hamsa (swan) sleeping close by. Fascinated by its beauty, he captures the sleeping bird which, waking in terror, laments that the king is attempting to kill him and that this will bring great misery to his widowed old mother and young wife. King Naḷa releases the swan and, assuring the bird that he has no evil intentions, sets him free. The bird flies away to its nest. Having once again tasted freedom, he feels that the king should be rewarded in some way for his magnanimity.

The swan comes back without fear and tells the king of the great qualities of Damayantī. He assures Naḷa that he has skill enough to bring about their union, if the king will permit it. King Naḷa is overjoyed and begs the swan to go quickly and tell Damayantī of his deep love for her. The swan flies away while the anxious king watches the bird disappearing in the distant horizon.

Scene IV. Damayantī, Her Companions, and the Hamsa
Damayantī is restless with the burden of her secret love for Naḷa. She comes to her garden with her companions. She soon finds the garden unbearable with its honey-sucking bees, the sweet singing birds and the perfume of flowers. Her companions are startled at her suggestion to leave the garden so soon. When she is about to leave, her attention is attracted by a lightning-like radiance. To her amazement, a golden swan alights near her. Marvelling at this rare swan, she desires to possess it. The bird cleverly moves on, decoying her to a safe distance from her companions and then tells her how childish she appears, chasing a bird.

Cleverly, the bird comes to the point by saying that he lives in the city of King Naḷa teaching the lovely damsels there how to acquire a graceful gait. Her curiosity and secret desire aroused, Damayantī is eager to know more about Naḷa from the bird.

The swan then asks her on whom her heart is set. He assures her that he will never betray her confidence and may be able to aid her. Damayantī, shedding her timidity and feeling that this rare swan is some divine creature, tells him of her love for Naḷa. She begs that he will go and tell her beloved how miserable she is. The swan agrees to convey her message, but asks Damayantī for her promise that she will not change her mind and marry another prince of her father's choice for that would not only render all his efforts fruitless, but also bring disgrace upon his kind. Damayantī assures the golden swan repeatedly of her unchanging love for Naḷa. The swan then promises that she will soon attain the fulfillment of her desire, and flies swiftly back to the court of King Naḷa.

Scene V. King Naḷa and the Hamsa
The swan returning to Naḷa tells him the precious news. The young king is overjoyed. Again and again he asks the golden swan to repeat to him the words of Damayantī. They are like nectar to his ears. At last the swan takes leave of him, promising that all will be well and that soon the marriage will be celebrated.

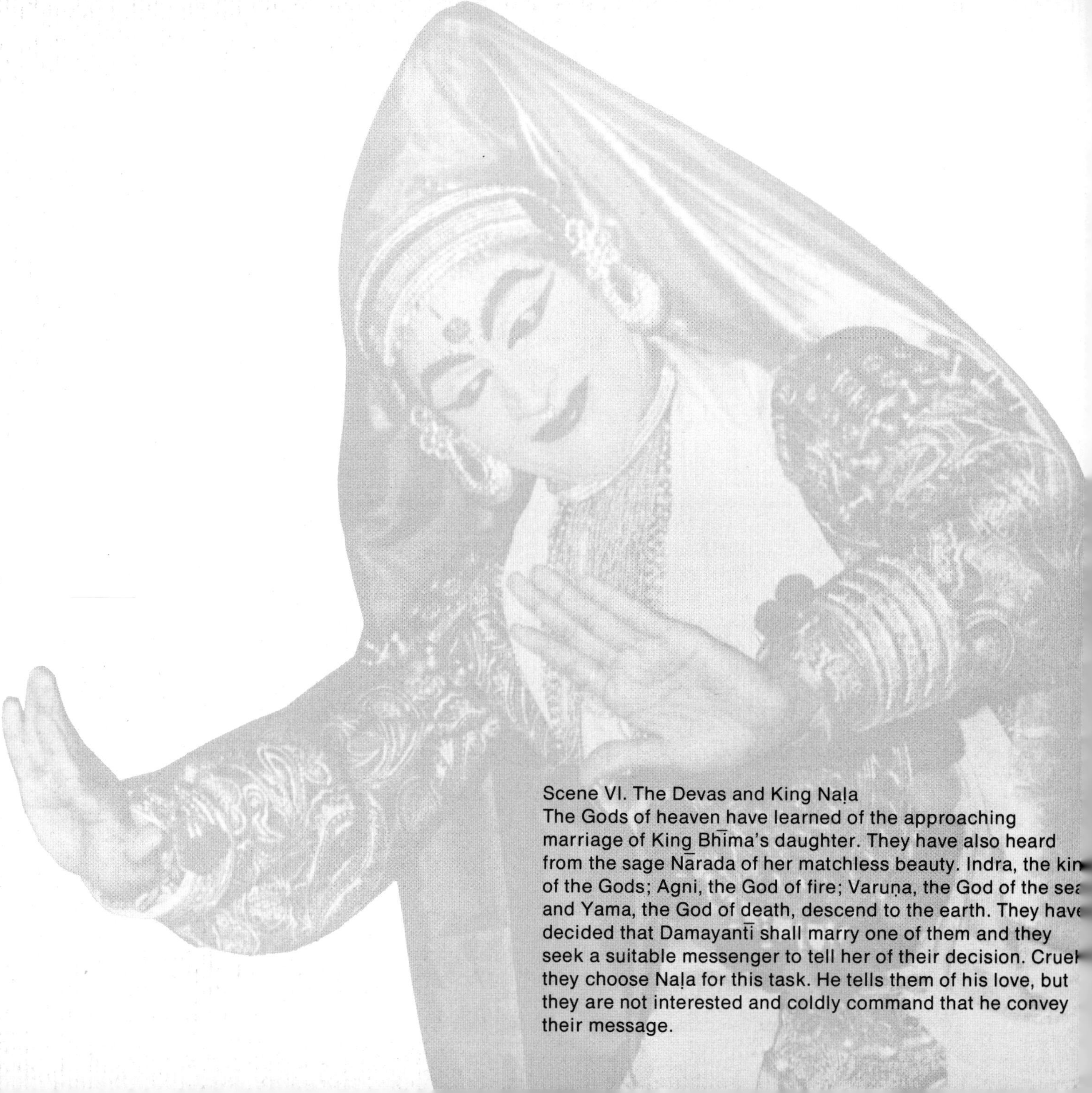

Scene VI. The Devas and King Naḷa

The Gods of heaven have learned of the approaching marriage of King Bhīma's daughter. They have also heard from the sage Nārada of her matchless beauty. Indra, the kin of the Gods; Agni, the God of fire; Varuṇa, the God of the sea and Yama, the God of death, descend to the earth. They hav decided that Damayantī shall marry one of them and they seek a suitable messenger to tell her of their decision. Cruel they choose Naḷa for this task. He tells them of his love, but they are not interested and coldly command that he convey their message.

e VII. King Naḷa and Damayantī
the help of the Gods, Naḷa quickly reaches Vidharba. He
s the great city, seeks out the court, and delivers to
ıyantī the message of the Gods. Damayantī recognizes
ıessenger as the man she loves and finally Naḷa admits
entity. Damayantī asks Naḷa to tell the Gods that she has
dy chosen Naḷa as her husband.

e VIII. King Bhīma's Court
hearing Damayantī's decision, the Gods determine to
ar at the ceremony at which Damayantī must choose her
ınd. They decide to magically appear each in the
cal form of Naḷa. Before King Bhīma's court, Damayantī
sees five kings all looking exactly like her future husband. She is terribly confused but realizes that one of them must be her own beloved Naḷa. Praying for guidance and firm in her faith, she approaches the five Naḷas and places the wedding garland unerringly on the real Naḷa. The Gods are pleased with her choice because it demonstrates the constancy of her love and faith. They shower the young couple with gifts; the Goddess Sarasvatī appears and blesses the couple; the swan appears to give them his blessing. From heaven the celestial hosts shower divine flowers down upon the happy pair. Conch shells sound and drums announce the auspicious event to the world.

There ends the First Day's Story.

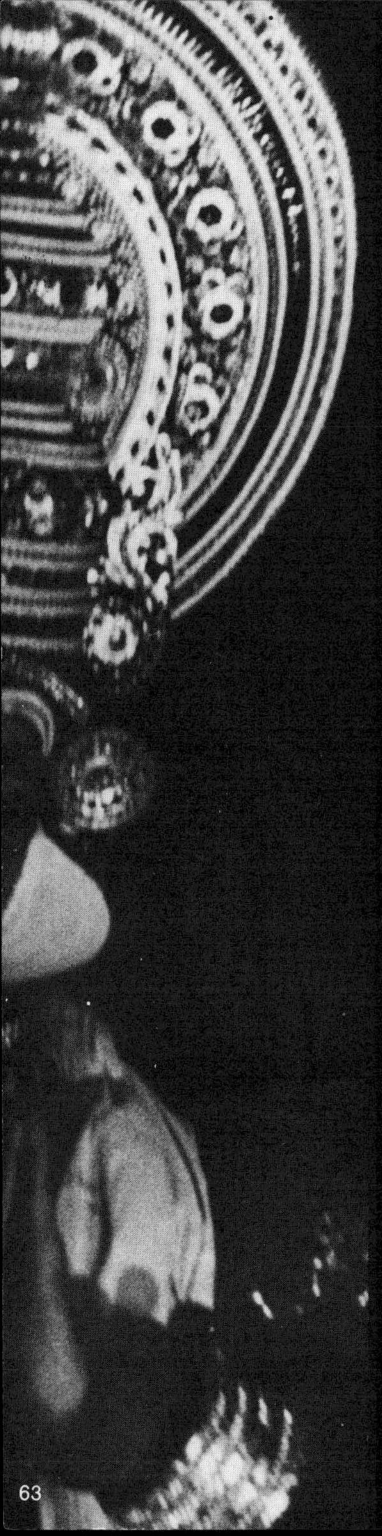

KIRĀTAM

(This episode is from the Vanaparvan of the Mahābhārata. While the Pāṇḍavas are living in exile in the forest with Draupadī, their wife, Arjuna, on the advice of the holy sage Vyāsa, goes to the mountain peak of Indraśaila near Mount Kailāsa, the home of Lord Śiva. He hopes to procure from Lord Śiva the divine arrow, the Pāśupatāstra, to help him and his brothers in their coming war against the Kauravas.)

Scene I. Arjuna's Penance
Arjuna undergoes religious penance to win the grace of Lord Śiva.

Scene II. Kāṭṭāḷan, Kāṭṭāḷatti, and the Bhūtas
Śiva has disguised himself as a Kāṭṭāḷan, a forest man or aboriginal hunter. Pārvatī has disguised herself as a Kāṭṭāḷatti, the wife of the hunter. In jovial humor, they admire each other's disguise. Then Śiva summons his bhūtas, mischievous spirits who live in the jungle, and they all set off to find Arjuna. Śiva wants to test his prowess and humble his pride a bit before giving him the Pāśupatāstra. Pārvatī insists that he promise not to harm the brave young Pāṇḍava.

Scene III. The Battle
Arjuna is absorbed in deep meditation on Lord Śiva. Duryodhana, the enemy of Arjuna, has sent a wild boar to kill him. Just as the boar is about to attack Arjuna, Kāṭṭāḷan, along with Kāṭṭāḷatti and the bhūtas, arrives on the scene. At the last moment Kāṭṭāḷan shoots an arrow at the boar; Arjuna, disturbed from his meditation, also sends an arrow at the boar and both arrows strike the animal simultaneously.

It is against the code of honour of a hunter to wound an animal that has already been shot by another. Kaṭṭāḷan taunts Arjuna and they begin an argument which rapidly develops into a battle. Taunts and challenges fill the air. Kaṭṭāḷan expresses the greatest contempt for the five Pāṇḍavas and their family; he insists they can scarcely be called respectable since each of the five has a different father. (Owing to a curse, the husband of their mother, Kuntī, was unable to consummate their marriage. A boon given her by a holy sage made it possible for her to conceive by various deities; hence Arjuna is the son of Indra, king of the Gods. Bhīma is the son of Vāyu, the wind God; Yudhiṣṭhira the son of Yama, the God of death. The twins, Nakula and Sahadeva, are the sons of the Aśvins, the twin deities of dawn and twilight.) Arjuna then swears by Lord Kṛiṣṇa that he will kill the forest man; Kaṭṭāḷan counters by saying that Kṛiṣṇa is a born thief, a stealer of milk and curds and even of ladies' clothes! (His remarks refer to well known stories about Kṛiṣṇa, relating how he stole into the houses of the cowherds and broke earthen pots containing butter, curd, and milk. Once, while the wives of the cowherds were bathing in the River Kālindī, Śrī Kṛiṣṇa removed their garments which were lying on the banks of the river. He then climbed up a nearby banyan tree and hung the garments there. When the ladies finished bathing and wanted to come out of the water, they were shocked to find their garments missing. Looking around they saw Śrī Kṛiṣṇa sitting on a branch of the tree, playing his divine flute, and teasing them. He refused to return their clothes until they came to him in their unclothed state, hands folded in supplication. As with most of the stories of Kṛiṣṇa, this is given a philosophical interpretation, but Kaṭṭāḷan in teasing Arjuna puts the worst possible light on the episode.)

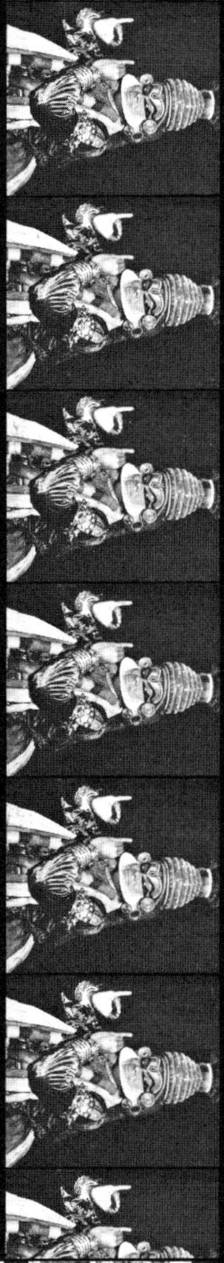

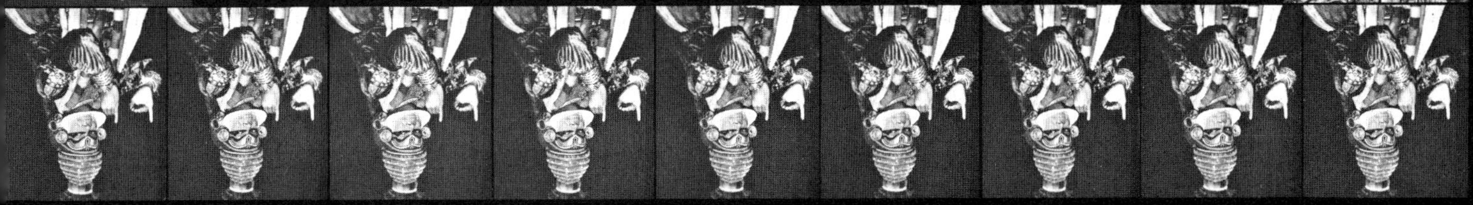

Kāṭṭāḷatti persists in trying to separate the combatants. She pleads with Kāṭṭāḷan to remember his promise not to harm Arjuna. She hints to Arjuna that this forest man is not what he seems. But both Arjuna and Kāṭṭāḷan are enjoying their battle and thrust her out of their way and ignore her. Finally she sends a curse at Arjuna that all of his arrows may turn into flowers. Arjuna is amazed to see the forest man covered with flowers. Finally Kāṭṭāḷatti, impatient for this battle to end, curses Arjuna that his quiver may be empty of arrows. Angry and surprised, he advances to Kāṭṭāḷan, in his fury intending to strike him with the bow itself. But the Goddess Gaṅgā (who resides in the tangled and matted locks of Śiva's hair) magically takes the bow away from him. Frustrated and furious, he determines to kill the forest man with his bare hands. They grapple and struggle until finally Arjuna is defeated and falls senseless to the ground. At Kāṭṭāḷatti's pleading, Kāṭṭāḷan magically heals all of Arjuna's wounds and revives him. They leave the stage.

Arjuna, regaining consciousness, makes a liṅga (Śiva's symbol) of earth and prepares to worship it. Belatedly, he realizes that the forest man was Śiva himself in disguise. Śiva and Pārvatī appear to him in their celestial forms. They comfort him and give him the boon he seeks. Slowly, to the sound of conch and drums, the divine pair ascend to their celestial abode.
Dhanāśi. Performed by Arjuna.

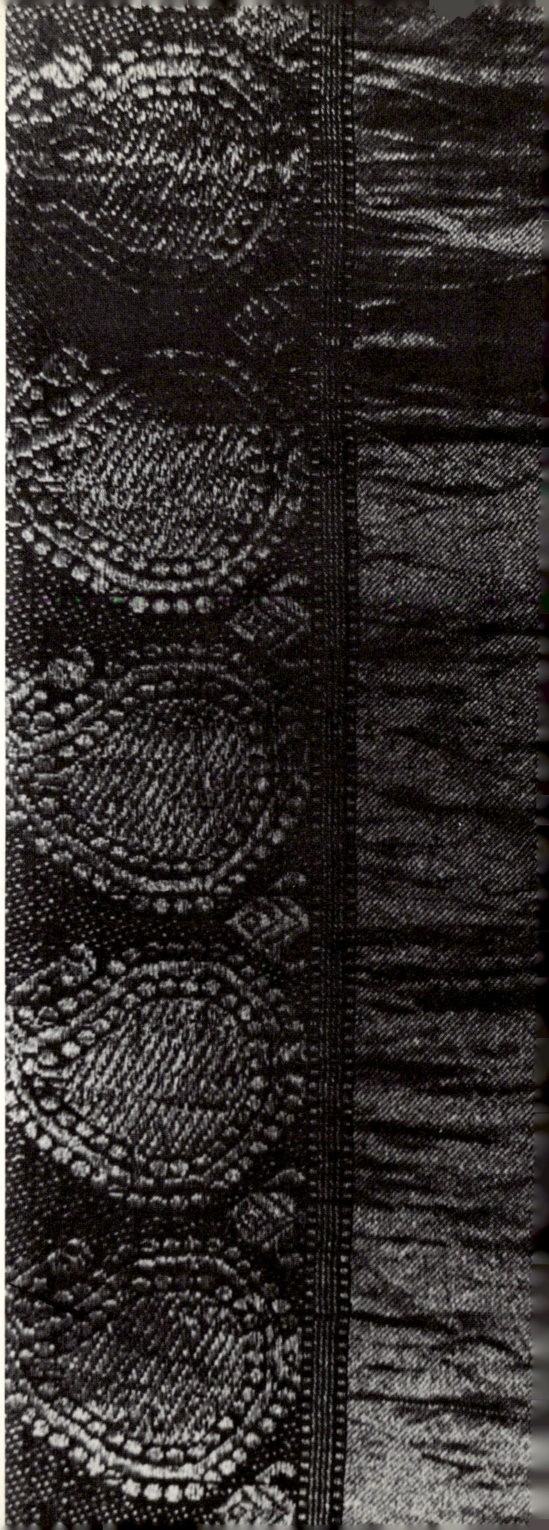

KALYĀṆA SAUGANDHIKAM

(This story is also from the Mahābhārata. It takes place while Arjuna has gone off in search of the Pāśupatāstra.)

Scene I. Bhīma and Draupadī

One day Bhīma and Draupadī are alone in the forest hermitage. A lovely flower is blown by the breeze and falls at Draupadī's feet. So charmed is she with its fragrance and beauty, she shows it to Bhīma. Flattering him a bit, she hints that if he is really fond of her, he will see that she gets more of these lovely flowers. Bhīma, glad of the opportunity to go off into the wild jungle on a dangerous mission, assures her that he will find the flowers for her, whether they be in heaven or on a mountaintop. As he is about to leave, Draupadī asks anxiously who will help him to defeat any enemies he may meet; he replies that his special weapon, his mace (gada), will be sufficient. When she asks what he will do for food and water, he replies that the memory of her loving glances will serve him for all sustenance.

Scene II. In the Forest

As Bhīma proceeds on the journey, he describes the wild forest through which he is passing (interpolation called vana varṇṇana or "description of the forest"). Vast stretches of forest land rugged with mountains and hills and infested with wild beasts lie before him. He describes the streams and valleys, a forest fire. He sees a lordly elephant roaming the jungle, tearing down branches from trees that stand in his path. The elephant is attacked by a huge python and then by a lion; the elephant, helpless and suffering, dies, and is swallowed by the python. (The story of the elephant is an optional interpolation and is called "Ajagarakabaḷitam.")

ene III. Hanumān and Bhīma

ıumān is sitting in the forest, lost in deep meditation. His d is fixed on Śrī Rāma. Presently he is disturbed by a loud se; he opens his eyes and looks for the cause. He sees hing unusual and resumes his meditation. This happens in and again; finally he is much annoyed. He wonders ether this great noise like thunder might be the mountains, ıg about and jostling one another in the sky. But no, he ıembers that Indra long ago cut off their wings and forced m to lead a more sedentary existence. He notices that all ıe animals are fleeing through the forest; even the lions e sought refuge in their caves.

hrough his powers of perception, Hanumān realizes that the ause of all the disturbance is some warrior striding through he forest, uprooting trees and frightening all the animals. He urther perceives that it is indeed his half-brother, Bhīma both are the sons of Vāyu, the Wind God). He decides to have little joke and to test Bhīma's strength before disclosing his dentity. He magically assumes the form of an old and ecrepit monkey and lies across the path.

hīma, tearing aside the trees of the thick jungle to clear his ath and making his way with long and stately strides, stops uddenly as he sees the old monkey. He shouts to the ionkey to move out of his way and threatens to throw him side. The monkey, pleading his aged and decrepit state, ays he cannot move; he warns Bhīma that he should not go iat way in any case, and should go back the way he came. hīma is indignant and increasingly vociferous; finally the ionkey suggests that he simply jump over him. But Bhīma eclines on the grounds that the monkey is of the same race s Hanumān, his own brother, and he would not therefore ommit this breach of etiquette. The monkey then invites him tell him more of this great monkey chieftain Hanumān, and hīma relates some of Hanumān's deeds and speaks of his alor and strength.

he monkey still declines to move and suggests that Bhīma ould move his tail and clear the way. To Bhīma's amazement, iough he tries with all his strength, he cannot at all move the il. Finally, in chastened mood, his pride humbled, Bhīma alizes this is no ordinary monkey. He begs the old monkey reveal his identity, and is delighted to hear it is indeed his alf-brother, the famous Hanumān. Bhīma begs to be forgiven s boorish behavior and asks if he may see the divine form which Hanumān jumped over the ocean, from the tip of dia to Ceylon, in search of Sītā. As Hanumān's form creases until it seems to fill the landscape, Bhīma is finally iable to bear the sight and loses consciousness.

anumān quickly resumes his normal form and revives his other, embracing him. He inquires about Bhīma's wife and others, and tells him how to find the Saugandhikam owers, blessing the journey. As Bhīma is about to leave and ntinue on his mission, he realizes that Hanumān has his ida. He must have his weapon with him, but feels a bit olish about asking for it. Hanumān lets him suffer for a bit, d finally returns the weapon (not without a rather sarcastic iile) and sends him on his way.

Dhanāśi. Performed by Bhīma.

CHOREOGRAPHIC STRUCTURE

The āṭṭakatha or poetic text for a Kathakaḷi dance-drama is arranged so that each scene of the story begins with a verse called ślokam or daṇḍakam (the terms refer to the meter of the poetry). The ślokam or daṇḍakam is sung, not in strict rhythm, but rather in anibaddha style, without percussion accompaniment. A ślokam or daṇḍakam occurs also before each padam within a scene. It is sometimes acted and sometimes not, as the dramatic action requires; it is in third person and, through descriptive or introductory means, gives the context and "sets the stage" for the padam to follow. The padam itself, usually consisting of pallavi, anupallavi, and caraṇams, is in first person as if the actor himself were speaking. The stylized gestures or mudrās closely follow the words of the text; there are even gestures to show grammatical suffixes. The mudrās involve not only the hands and arms; they are coordinated with movement of the entire body — feet, legs, torso, head, eyes, eyebrows, and appropriate facial expression. The pallavi, anupallavi, and each caraṇam are repeated by sections, usually two or three times, before the gestures for that line are complete and the next line is taken up; the "punctuation" between each line is the kalāśam. Though a kalāśam is a passage of dance, it cannot properly be called "pure dance." It is rather dramatic dance since the bhāva or emotional mood must be continued throughout, not only by the facial expression, but also by the manner in which the movements are executed. In addition, mudrās are sometimes shown during parts of the kalāśam. The first words of the pallavi, sometimes the entire pallavi or a caraṇam, may be sung during part of the kalāśam; otherwise it is performed to percussion alone.

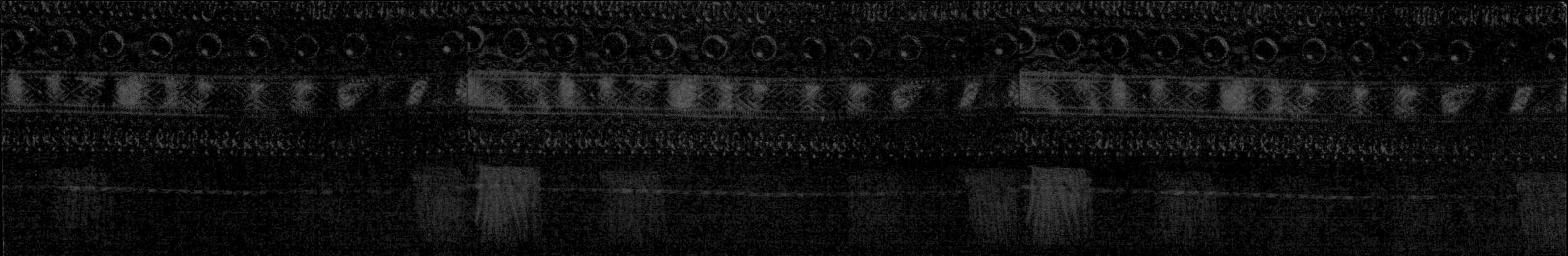

The system of kalāśams is complex and meticulous. Theoretically, the kalāśam used in each instance depends upon the character being portrayed, the situation according to the story line, the tāla or rhythmic pattern, and the kāla or tempo. Given all these, the Kathakaḷi actor knows which variety of kalāśam must be used. There are some stories, however, in which many of the kalāśams are specially choreographed. These stories are said to have "colliyāṭṭam," "spoken action" or "dancing the words." The term is also used in the sense of "rehearsal." These colliyāṭṭam stories (there are seventeen, of which some have only partial colliyāṭṭam) have set traditional choreography (plus opportunities for improvisation at specified junctures) and are learned in detail by students and carefully rehearsed as part of the continuing studio practice. The other stories which have no colliyāṭṭam are learned by memorizing the āṭṭakatha (it is obvious which gestures are to be used since the gesture language of Kathakaḷi is fully codified) and by repeatedly watching the Āśāns (teachers and masters of the art) in actual performance. So firm is the basic choreographic structure of Kathakaḷi that these non-colliyāṭṭam stories are as well performed as the seventeen rehearsed stories and often gain in spontaneity. The colliyāṭṭam stories often have the most interestingly choreographed kalāśams, whereas the other stories permit much greater freedom of interpretation.

Ordinarily a kalāśam occurs after two or three repetitions of a line of the padam; sometimes it occurs before the line of the text; sometimes there is a kalāśam "on each side" of a line of text. Sometimes it involves additional dance passages called aṭakkam and tōṅkāram. These additions or extensions of the kalāśam illustrate a principle often used in Kerala music: just as a phrase is about to come to an end, the last beat is unexpectedly taken as the first beat of another phrase.

In the iraṭṭi kalāśams ("doubled" kalāśams), of which there are several varieties, the movements are graceful, lending themselves to the emotions of compassion, desire, and to a mild and dignified form of heroism. Valiya kalāśaṁs ("big" kalāśams) are used only in male roles, particularly in scenes where the predominant emotion is rage or heroism. Vaṭṭam vaccu kalāśams ("circle" kalāśams) also occur only in male roles. They are generally in a slower tempo than valiya kalāśams and express a variety of emotional moods, including compassion and heroism. Aṣṭa kalāśam ("eight" kalāśam) is in a rhythm of ten beats (campa tāla). There is only one aṣṭa kalāśam; it is lengthy and vigorous with many complex variations of the rhythmic pattern. In the Kalluvazhi sampradāyam, the tradition followed at Kerala Kalamandalam, it occurs in its full form only in "Kālakēya Vadham" when Arjuna, the Pāṇḍava hero, expresses his joyful amazement at finding himself in Heaven where he has been summoned by his illustrious father, Indra, King of the Gods. In 1967 this kalāśam was used for the first time in another Kathakaḷi dance-drama, "Subhadrā Haraṇam." Balabhadra (performed by Vazhenkata Kunjan Nayar Āśān) and Kṛiṣṇa (performed by T. T. Ramankutti Nayar Āśān) are delighted and astonished by a marvelous feat by Arjuna. An enormous army was sent to intercept Arjuna and to prevent his carrying off Subhadrā to be his bride. But the mighty warrior, by his unprecedented skill, left the army helpless though unharmed. The use of aṣṭa kalāśam performed by both actors in this instance was well received by the "Kathakaḷi bhrāntan" and bids fair to become a permanent part of that particular scene.

This does not at all exhaust the fascinating subject of kalāśams; there are many more varieties and much more to be said. However, a more thorough analysis of the subject must necessarily become highly technical.

There are in Kathakaḷi interpolated passages called iḷakiyāṭṭam or manōdharmma which are performed to percussion alone. Since there is no singing in these portions, the actors are freed from the necessity of following the text and theoretically they may improvise. In actual practice the interpolated passages range from completely improvised "soliloquies" or "conversations" (entirely in gesture of course) to passages which are traditionally set and are performed with strict adherence to a text specifically written for the purpose, even though it is not sung. The two terms are not precisely defined. Iḷakiyāṭṭam is often used to denote those passages which are traditionally set, but may also mean the improvised portions. Manōdharmma denotes only the free improvisation. These interpolations are in a rhythm of sixteen beats except for a few highly structured iḷakiyāṭṭams which are in a rhythm of seven beats.

In the context of Kathakaḷi, the word iḷakiyāṭṭam has two other uses as well. It is used to denote prescribed dance movements which accompany specific gestures, when they are performed by certain classes of characters. The word is used also for a kind of interpolation which occurs within a padam and elaborates upon a line or a portion of a line. The line or portion thereof is repeated an indefinite number of times until the elaboration is finished and the actor is ready to proceed to the next part of the text.

In addition to acting through stylized gesture, Kathakaḷi also employs pantomime with various degrees of realism.

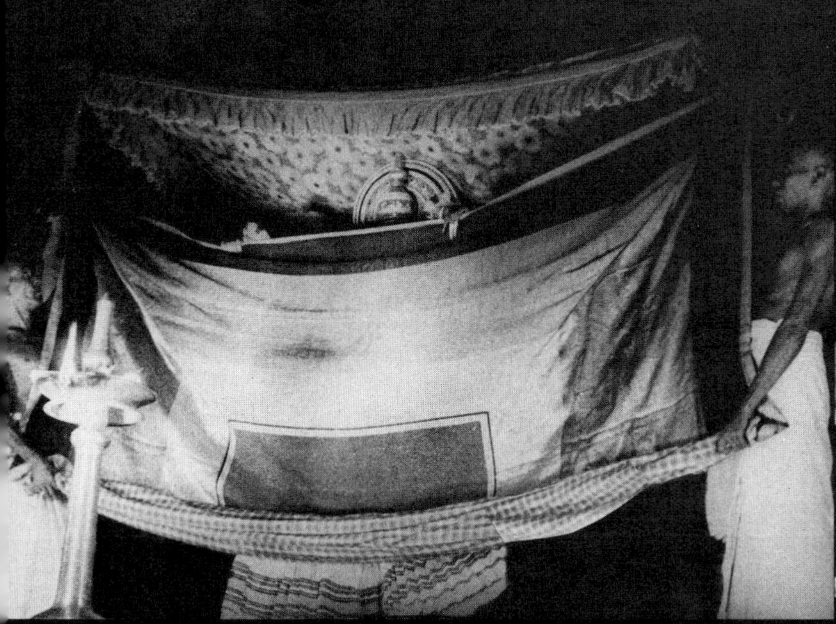

Entrances are achieved through use of the tiraśśīla, the Kathakaḷi curtain held by two men. The tiraśśīla varies in size (usually it is approximately six feet by nine feet) and in elegance. It is made up of concentric rectangles of different colors; red, green, yellow, and black are the most common. It may have the figure of a deity in the center, or the name of the troupe or yōgam in the very decorative Malayalam script.

For ordinary entrances the men holding the curtain simply remove it. For the first entrance of a character whose nature is excessively proud, evil, dangerous, villainous, rough and rowdy, or for an animal character (katti, cukannattāṭi, veḷḷattāṭi, etc.) a passage called tiranōkku (performed to percussion alone) establishes his personality before he begins the scene. The tiraśśīla is lowered only part of the way. The actor grasps it; it trembles, vibrates, billows as pulls it this way and that; he poses, fixing the audience w a piercing stare; he moves upstage and then comes forw again near the kaḷi viḷakku, the four-foot-high oil and wic lamp which provided the sole lighting for Kathakaḷi befo the advent of the Coleman lantern and electricity. (The k viḷakku is still considered a necessary adjunct to the performance. It symbolizes Śiva and is respectfully salu by the actor who performs the Dhanāśi, the auspicious closing dance.) In the tiranōkku, as the actor vigorously manipulates the curtain, he may fan the flame of the lam that the brightly burning wick heightens the effect of the makeup, the stylized eye movements, the glittering kirīṭ or crown — a stunning use of the simplest of "equipmer

the tiranōkku, as well as elsewhere in the drama, the actor ıploys alarcca, inarticulate vocal sounds which are in ꞓping with the character portrayed. For example an actor a katti role such as Rāvaṇa will utter the syllable "Gve-e-e," staining the "e." This will be in a voice between speech and ging; the syllable will be repeated by the actor in the tonic, h, and octave. The form of alarcca used for Hanumān is yyaha!" Kāṭṭāḷan, the "forest man" in "Kirātam," emits e cries of "Po po!" in a high falsetto voice, reminiscent of sound of a bird or small animal in the jungle. Like the ınōkku, alarcca is never used for the more refined ıracters such as pacca, minukku, etc.

ꞓ tiranōkku is fairly simple in its construction, but is a little n of choreography, allowing for variations. The character portrayed and the bhāva or mood greatly affect the manner in which it is performed.

The term tiranōkku should not be confused with nōkku; the latter signifies a partial lowering of the curtain so that the actor (sometimes more than one) may be seen before his first full appearance. A good example occurs at the beginning of Puṟappāṭu. The nōkku is a great deal simpler than tiranōkku and is often used for refined characters such as pacca (heroes, virtuous kings, deities).

This is a brief and very general outline of the choreographic structure of Kathakaḷi. If we examine several stories in detail, we will find a great many variations, all of them aimed at the complete dramatic visualization of the epic stories.

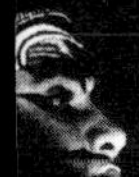

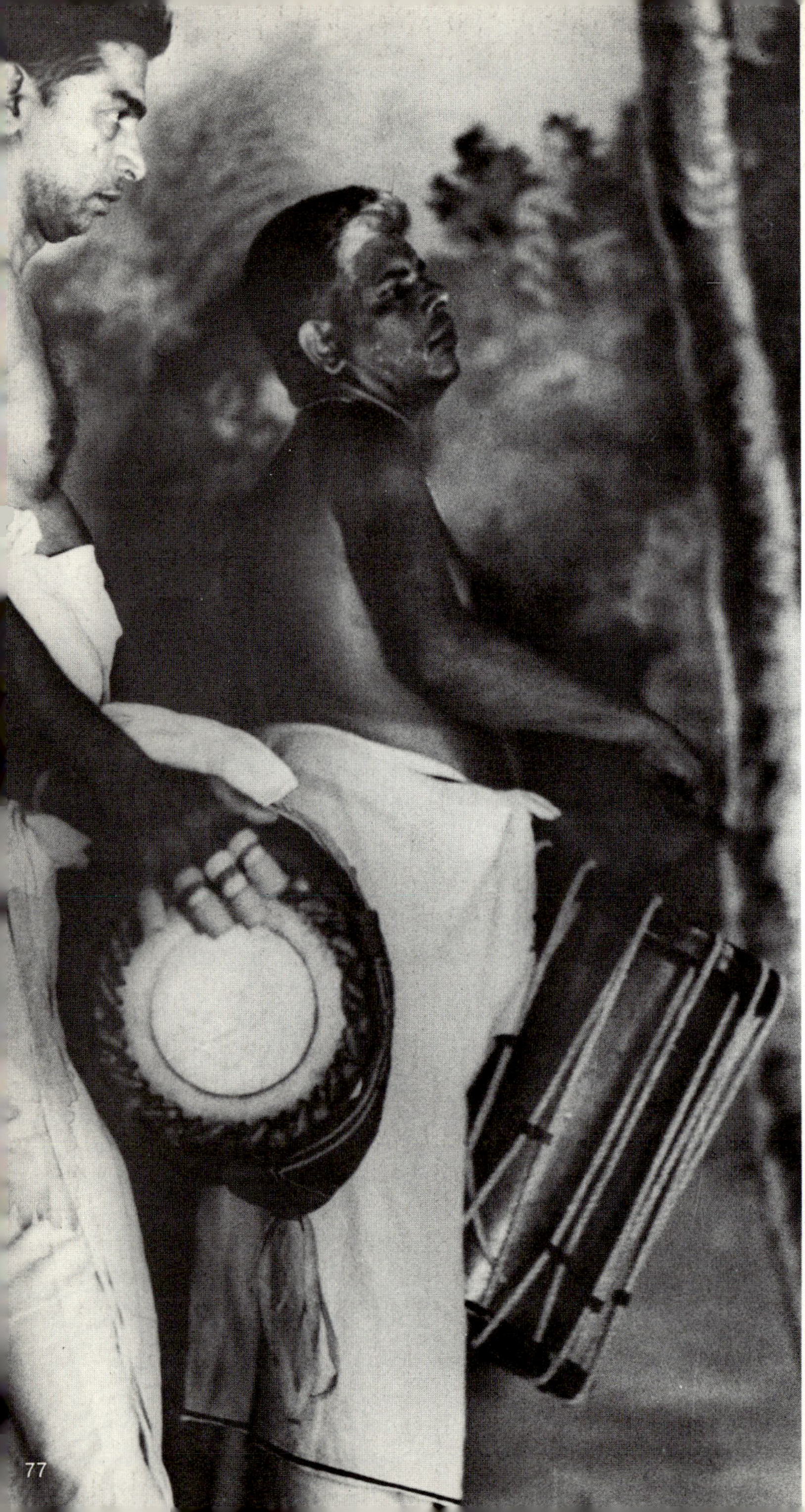

MUSICAL ACCOMPANIMENT

Two singers and two drummers provide the accompanimen for Kathakaḷi. The first singer (ponnāni) keeps the steady b of the tāla (rhythmic pattern) by using the cēṅṅalam, a gon of the famous Kerala bell-metal, held in the left hand and beaten with a stick held in the right. The second singer (śaṅkiṭi) follows the first singer and also keeps the tāla by using ilattāḷam, a pair of large bell-metal hand cymbals. Th style of singing is known as the "sōpāna style"; the word sōpāna means "stairs" and the phrase "sōpāna style" is derived from the singing during ritual celebration at the steps of the sanctum of the temple. Though related to Karn classical music, the Kerala sōpāna style is a special development. Particularly in Kathakaḷi, the vocal style is m "operatic," expansive and dramatic. The clarity of the text and the creation of bhāva or emotional mood are of prime importance.

The śuddha maddaḷam is a double-headed drum of some three to three and one-half feet in length; it is barrel shape similar to the mṛidaṅgam of Tamilnad. The śuddha madda is usually made of jack wood; the head at the right end is o ox hide, the left of buffalo hide. The left side has a black sp similar to that on the right side of the mṛidaṅgam. The maddaḷam is hung in a horizontal position by a cloth which passes at the back of the waist. It is played only with the hands, and the right hand has finger stalls made of a mixtu of rice paste and cuṇṇam (calcinated shell lime), applied t strips of cloth, wound about the fingers, and allowed to harden. The sound produced is particularly melodious with ringing overtones. In Kathakaḷi the śuddha maddaḷam is us for all padams, regardless of which class of character is being portrayed. The first sound of a Kathakaḷi performanc is provided by the maddaḷam as the drummer plays the cōriṭṭu kai, an exceptionally beautiful, composed piece of percussion for śuddha maddaḷam alone.

The ceṇṭa is used along with the śuddha maddaḷam for padams by male characters, or by a demoness, but never f other female characters. It is a tall cylindrical drum, somewhat less than three feet in length, usually made of ja wood and covered on both sides with cow hide. Tension cords passing through loops or rings are used to heighten or lower the pitch in tuning. The left end or iṭantala is cove with one piece of leather; the right end or valantala has si seven additional circles of leather of diminishing diameters glued on the inside. Ordinarily in Kathakaḷi, the iṭantala is played; at certain dramatic moments, particularly when a deity assumes his cosmic form or interferes in human affairs, the valantala is played. The valantala is used also for certain of the Tantrik rituals of Kerala temples. The ceṇṭa is played either with one hand and one stick or with two sticks. Perhaps the most striking use of the ceṇṭa in Kerala is for tāyambaka, a highly complex percussion composition for one lead ceṇṭa, four accompanying ceṇṭas, and two or three ilattāḷam. The ayambaka, one to one and a half hours in duration, is often heard at temple festivals and other celebrations. It is in five movements and is in campaṭa tāla (sixteen beats) throughout, although three other tālas found in Kerala (aṭanta, fourteen eats; campa, ten beats; and pañcāri, six beats) are superimposed on the sixteen beats of campaṭa. The ceṇṭa as a sharp metallic sound, especially effective in scenes of attle where the emotional mood involves rage or heroism. is also capable of producing a delicate murmur as well as umming or whirring sounds, effective counterparts of elicate movements of the actor's hands and eyes.

he iṭekka, according to legend, was sent to earth by Lord iva. Shaped like an hour glass, the iṭekka has two heads, ach covered with an animal membrane. In length the drum about twelve to fourteen inches. It has tension strings hich are manipulated with the left hand as the head is eaten with a curved slender stick, usually of sandal wood, eld in the right hand. Through manipulation of the tension ords, all the notes of the octave can be played, and even ore than one full octave can be achieved by an accomplished usician. The iṭekka is fully collapsible and is taken apart hen not in use. Both the ceṇṭa and iṭekka are hung by a cloth hich passes over the left shoulder; very often a musician ill be well versed in both these instruments. In Kathakaḷi e iṭekka is used along with the maddaḷam for padams in hich female characters are portrayed.

ne blowing of a conch shell (śamkhu) heightens the amatic impact of special important moments in Kathakaḷi. enerally it is used when the valantala of the ceṇṭa is played; ke the valantala, it is also used in temple ritual. The mewhat eerie note of the conch lends an air of significance, portentous events. Beginning softly as if in the distance, owly the single note swells until it seems to fill the air and be the very voice of the celestial beings of the epics.

THE USE OF TĀLA AND RĀGA IN DRAMATIC ACTION

The intricate and ingenious use of rhythm or tāla (Sanskrit; the Malayalam word is tāḷam) is one of the most appealing features of Indian music. When applied to the various forms of Indian dance and dance-drama, tāla becomes increasingly critical. A specific tāla may be defined as a rhythmic pattern, its character determined by the length of the tāḷavaṭṭam (a Malayalam word meaning one complete cycle of the rhythmic pattern) and by the arrangement of strong, medium, and light accents. The length of the tāḷavaṭṭam will be governed by the number of mātras, a word which signifies a unit of time.

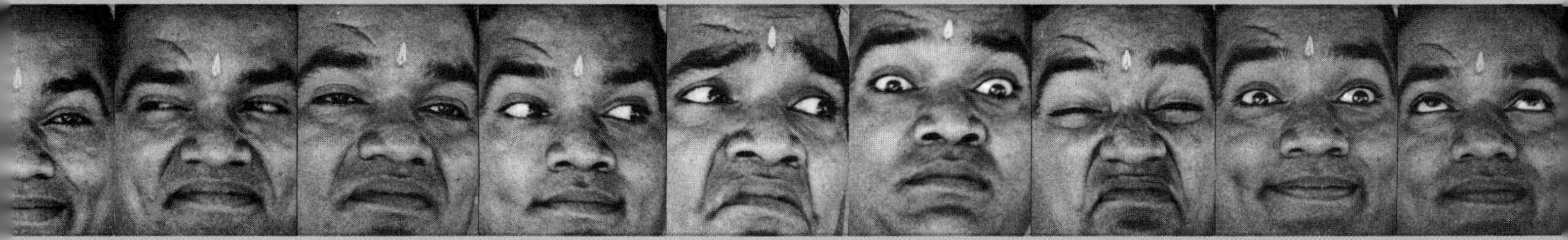

BHĀVA HĀSA BHĀVA ŚOKA BHĀVA UTSĀHA BHĀVA BHAYA BHĀVA KRODHA BHĀVA JUGUPSĀ BHĀVA VISMAYA BHĀVA ŚAMA BHĀVA

In Kathakaḻi only six tālas are in use. These are campaṭa (sixteen mātras), aṭanta (fourteen), campa (ten), tripuṭa (seven), muṟiyaṭanta (six) and pañcāri (six). These six tālas, in their various kālas or tempi, and used with appropriate rāgas, are sufficient to portray every mood required by this dance-drama form. The sources of Kathakaḻi's thematic material indicate how great the range of characters and situations may be. Drawn from the Mahābhārata, the Rāmāyaṇa, and other Puranic tales, the full sweep of Indian mythology and legend provides the framework for the stories. The nine sthāyibhāvas (dominant emotional moods) of Indian dramatic theory as well as the sañcāribhāvas (subordinate emotional states) find full scope.

One of the technique exercises of Kathakaḷi training, kāl sādhakam ("leg or foot practice"), employs six kālas or tempi. Ordinarily however in performance, five kālas are used. The slowest is called pati kāla and is the slowest kāla of tāyambaka, an intricate percussion composition heard at temple festivals. In Kathakaḷi pati kāla is used only for patiññāṭṭampadams, sometimes occurring in the first scene, sometimes later in the drama. It is often a tender love scene of which rati (love, desire, eroticism) is the sthāyibhāva; there may however be a different emotion predominating such as śoka (sorrow, compassion). Each gesture of a patiññāṭṭampadam has its fullest and most complex form; each movement is infinitely slow and detailed. The stylized facial expressions used to portray rati and śoka add greatly to the effectiveness of the mesmeric "slow motion" quality. Patiññāṭṭampadams are considered a supreme test of an actor's ability and the most highly classical and refined of Kathakaḷi padams.

Besides pati kāla, Kathakaḷi employs first, second, third, and fourth kālas. According to Indian musical theory second kāla is twice as fast as first, third is twice as fast as second, etc. These kālas are relative; first kāla in one instance may be slightly faster than in another. Once the kāla is established, however, if it is to be doubled, the doubling must be exact.

Kathakaḷi dance-dramas generally begin in a slow kāla, either pati kāla or first kāla; throughout the course of the drama the tempo gradually quickens. The tempo of an individual padam, however, is chosen with consideration to the dramatic values of that padam as well as to its place in the continuity of the drama as a whole. Variations in kāla may even occur within a padam if the bhāva will be thus heightened.

The most frequently occurring tāla is campaṭa; we can find examples of its use to portray the full range of bhāvas. Where dignity and majesty are required, aṭanta may be used; desire, pity, or heroism may be dominant. Scenes of tension, agitated dispute, or battle, often employ campa tāla. Tripuṭa is almost invariably used for padams by sages and often for padams by Brāhmaṇas. When Rāvaṇa in the Rāmāyaṇa appears to Sītā disguised as a holy man, his padams are in tripuṭa, third kāla. Her answering padams are in tripuṭa, second kāla. In "Naḷa Caritam, First Day's Story," Nārada as he tells Naḷa of Damayantī and her charms, uses tripuṭa in first kāla, somewhat slow and elaborate as befits his dignity and the nature of his errand. Tripuṭa is used also for scenes of tension. Both mur̲iyaṭanta and pañcāri have a short tāḷavaṭṭam and a lighthearted, almost comical swing. They often occur for kari vēṣam, the character of demoness who in Kathakaḷi sometimes portrays hāsa or comedy as well as jugupsā, the horrific, odious, or distasteful. Pañcāri is used also for specific actions where it fits particularly well, such as in "Kirātam" when Śiva, disguised as Kāṭṭāḷan, sharpens his sword. Mur̲iyaṭanta may also be used for a fast-moving scene in which anger or heroism is predominant.

The final scenes, especially those involving violence and the destruction of evil forces, are in campaṭa tāla, fourth kāla. Very often additional percussionists will add to the excitement of the final important apotheosis of the evening — all four drummers, who have worked in alternating pairs during the all-night-long performance, and actors who have finished their roles earlier in the evening, removed makeup and costume, and returned to the stage to play cymbals. The waves of sound, the insistence of the repeated short rhythmic phrase produce an arresting feeling of inevitability as well as satisfaction at the unfolding of the climactic denouement, just as the sun rises.

Like the tāla and the kāla, the rāga is also chosen with careful consideration to the bhāva and the character portrayed. We find that the same rāga may be used to portray a quite different emotion and situation if the tāla and kāla, and the delineation of the rāga itself, are altered. For example the rāga Khaṇṭāram, often used for katti vēṣam, may in one instance express utsāha or heroism, and in another, with appropriate changes, may equally well express śoka or compassion. Pāṭi rāga is always used for a patiññāṭṭampadam performed by katti, but is found occasionally elsewhere as well. Mōhana rāga is often used for bhakti or devotion. For kari vēṣam, the character of demoness, Saurāṣṭra rāga is usual.

A rāga may change within a padam to emphasize a change of bhāva. Although the published editions of āṭṭakatha[4] have the tālas and rāgas noted, these are not always accurate as far as present practice is concerned. Tradition, as it descends from teacher to student, dictates the rāga and tāla to be used in each instance. As the tradition itself has developed, no doubt these aspects have altered.

A detailed study of the rāgas used in Kathakaḷi is yet to be undertaken. An analysis on the basis of their use (with appropriate tāla and kāla) for scenes and characters of various categories, a comparison of rāgas in Kathakaḷi with rāgas of the same name in other areas of South India, a comparison with the svaras of Kūṭiyāṭṭam, used in the chanting of the lines of the Sanskrit drama — a study encompassing such aspects would broaden the scope of our knowledge of the music and the theatre of South India.

ACTING TECHNIQUES

Though an epic form of theatre, Kathakaḷi is not pageant-like or stereotyped. As we have discussed elsewhere, there are in Kathakaḷi classified character types immediately recognizable by their costuming, ornamentation, and makeup; however, details of makeup are subtly varied to conform to the specific individual character. Nuances of acting are similarly varied. An artistically valid portrayal of a role by a distinguished actor depends largely upon psychological interpretation of the character. The differences between one actor's portrayal of a role and another's, as well as between the interpretations of the same actor upon different occasions, provide one of the aesthetic delights of Kathakaḷi. Besides nuances of interpretation of the same material, there are sequences in every Kathakaḷi dance-drama where the actor is given scope for improvisation; thus, there is opportunity for the actor to employ his creative ability to the fullest extent. This principle of "variation within a set framework" is a cardinal rule of Indian art as a whole, and finds as real an expression in the dance-drama form of Kathakaḷi as in, for instance, Karnatic classical music, or a sculptor's or painter's rendering of the figure of a given deity.

The actor in Kathakaḷi, who incidentally is often incorrectly referred to as a dancer, does not "speak" except with his hands. The text of the drama is sung for him and is the base line of his interpretation. The two principal elements of the acting technique are mudrā or gesture and mukhābhinaya or facial expression. These two, combined with the mysterious quality which the West calls "projection of emotion" and which Indian dramatic theory speaks of as "sāttvikābhinaya," form the basis of the actor's art.

TRIPATĀKA

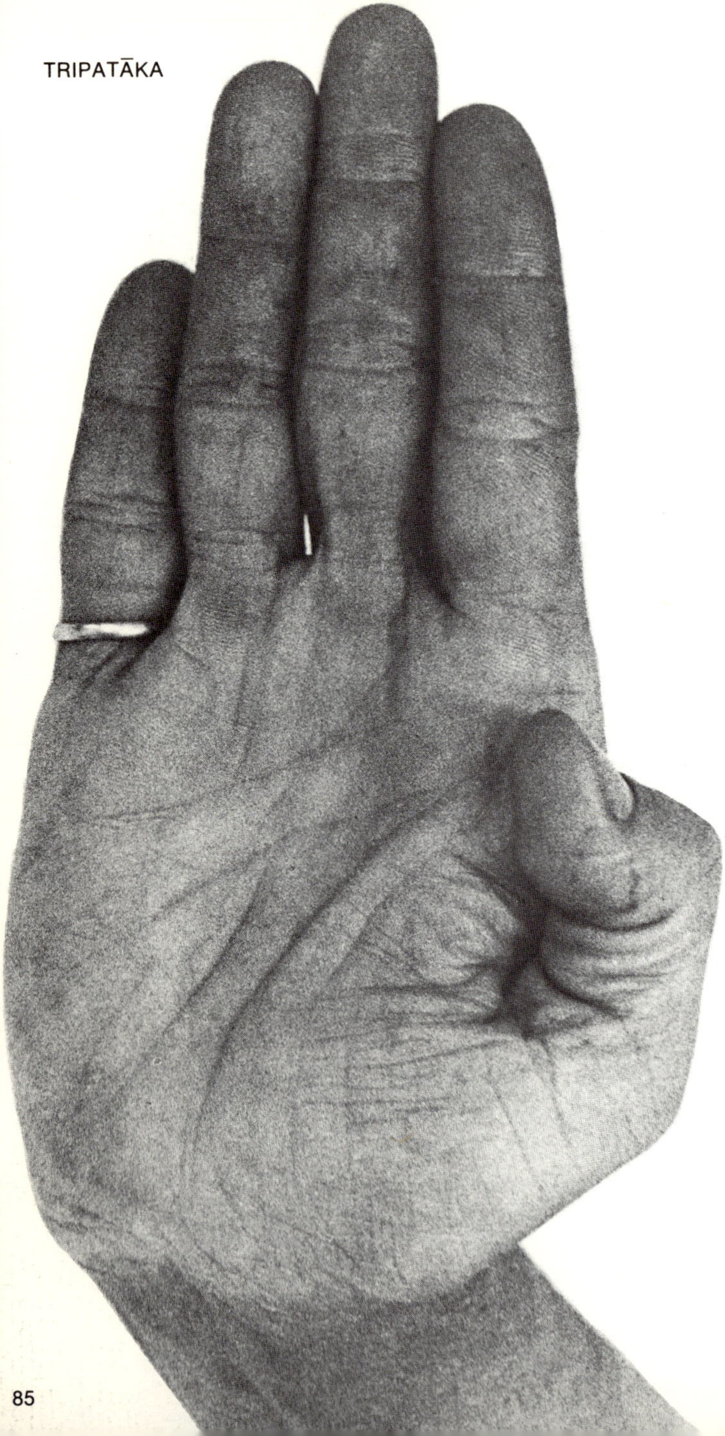

The mudrās of Kathakaḷi are highly codified; since they mus follow the text exactly, this is an obvious necessity. There are mudrās for nouns, for verbs, for adjectives, for adverbs, for prepositions, for suffixes denoting the infinitive, the conditional mood, the optative mood and the imperative, the plural, the adjective form, the locative, and for the case called by some linguists the "ablative of connection" (samyōjika), meaning "together with." There are mudrās fo pronouns, including the honorary third person pronoun. The vocative case is expressed by adding the gesture for "you" to the noun. There is even a mudrā which means the "end c a sentence." All of these follow the grammatical structure c Malayalam. So complete is the codification of gesture in Kathakaḷi that the poet Vallathol, when he became rather deaf in his later years, requested that his friends "speak" tc him through mudrās, and carried on a great part of his conversation in this manner. To be accurate, we must add that when a padam is in a very fast kāla, the "grammatical mudrās" are sometimes omitted, aesthetics being of greater importance than strict grammatical accuracy in such a case.

A mudrā in the sense of a "meaningful gesture" is not merely a "hand position"; it is a movement, involving one o more hand positions. There are twenty-four (there are actually more in use, but twenty-four in theory) basic hand positions which are used in mudrās. Some confusion arises over the fact that both the hand positions themselves, whic have no specific meaning, and the movement which does have a specific meaning, are both called mudrās. They are also both called hastas; the terms are interchangeable. Hasta means "hand"; mudrā means, in this context, "sign." But there is in actual usage no distinction between the two words. For the sake of clarity, the "meaningful gesture" wi be called herein mudrā or gesture; otherwise the phrase "hand pose" will be used.

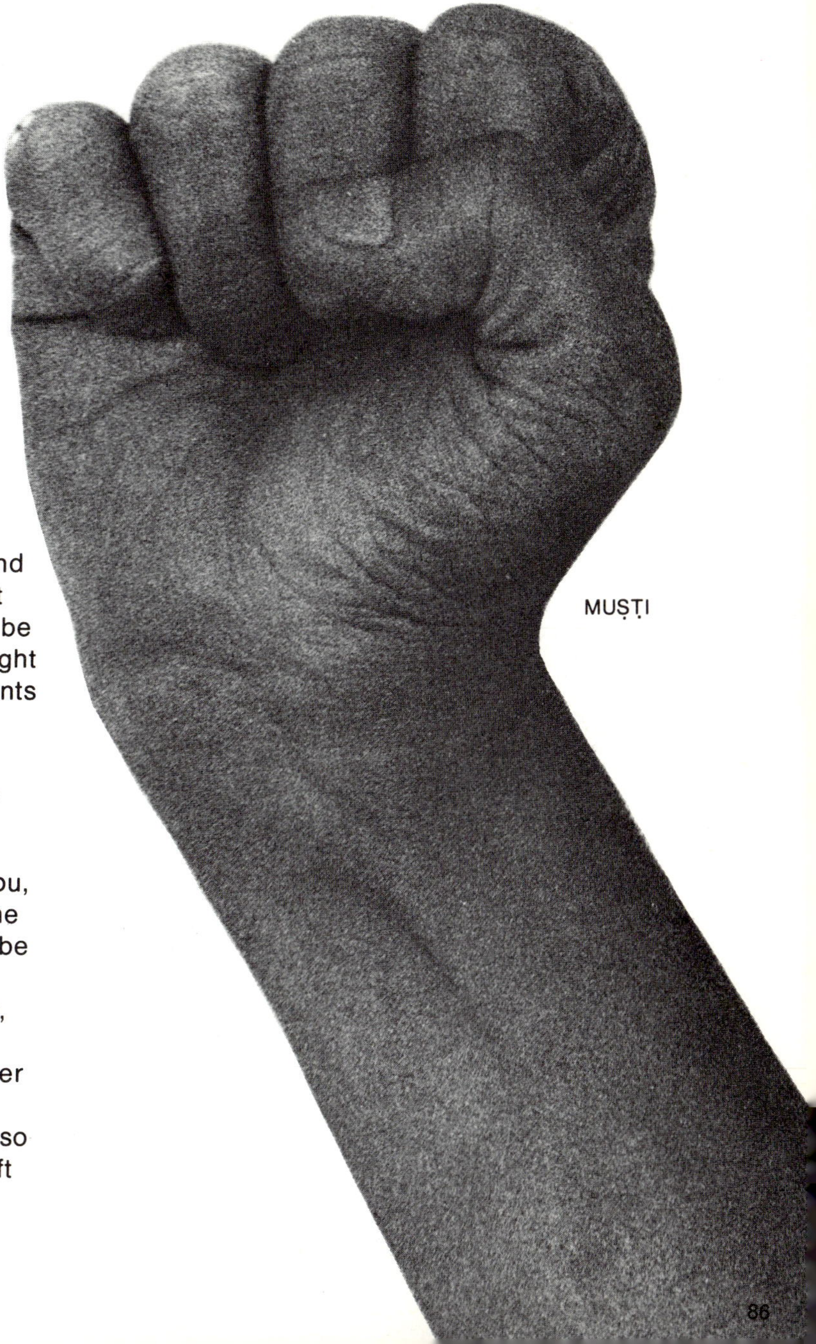

MUṢṬI

Some mudrās involve both hands and may be reversed, depending upon which side of the stage the character occupies (stage right is the "honored" side of the stage and is occupied by the more important character); others must not be reversed. Similarly, some single-hand mudrās may be done with either hand; some must be done only with the right hand, some only with the left. Every mudrā has eye movements which complement it; many have movements of the body, the legs and feet, including jumping movements, which accompany them. These latter accompanying movements, called iḷakiyāṭṭam, are not always used with the mudrā; it depends somewhat on the character portrayed, the story, etc. Circular movements of the upper torso, called cuzhippu, are however almost invariably present. Depending upon the bhāva or emotional mood, the cuzhippu may occasionally be reversed. For instance in the mudrā for "all" the hands describe a horizontal circle beginning in front of the chest, moving to the left, forward, to the right and back to the beginning position in front of the chest. Ordinarily the upper torso bends in this same pattern. However if the bhāva is utsāha (the heroic mood), the body movement is reversed so that the torso bends first to the right, then forward, then left and back to its normal position.

The theory of the eye movements provides an interesting footnote. There is a well-known statement in Abhinayadarpaṇam which has been translated thus:

> Where the hand goes, eyes also should go there.
> Where the eyes go, mind also should go there.
> Where the mind goes, there the State (bhāva)
> should follow,
> And where there is the State, there the Sentiment
> (rasa) arises.[5]

It is true that in other forms of Indian dance and dance-drama, the eyes usually follow the hand which is executing at any given moment the most important movement; the artist must actually look at the hand. In Kathakaḷi and in Kūṭiyāṭṭam, however, we have a different interpretation of this theory. When the hand makes a circular movement, the eyes do likewise. The actor does not look at the hand; the eyes imitate the movement of the hand and thereby emphasize it.

Detailed description of the hundreds of mudrās used in Kathakaḷi would be of little value to the layman. It is extraordinarily difficult to describe any movement in words. Photographs or drawings will show only certain fragmented poses from the continuity of a single mudrā, giving a very incomplete and ultimately unsatisfactory impression. To the reader, poring over pages and pages of laborious description even if pointed up with drawings or photographs, it would still be a thankless task, resulting in more confusion than enlightenment. A few references to types of mudrās, however, may be of interest.

There are three basic positions from which most Kathakaḷi gestures begin. These correspond to the Western ballet arm positions, first, fifth high, and fifth low. However, instead of the soft curve of the balletic arms, the Kathakaḷi positions are a "diamond shape," the arms bent at the elbows, the finger tips almost touching. We may find exceptions in mudrās which do not begin from one of these positions, but the rule is generally applicable.

There are "classes" or "sets" of gestures which seem to be related or derived from other gestures. A mudrā which denotes something soft will involve a patting motion. The mudrā for "soft" itself uses a patting movement of the thumb against the first two fingers (combined with other movement). The mudrā for "breasts" uses a trembling patting movement of the fingers. The mudrā for "soft young tendril" again uses a trembling patting motion as the tendril "grows" upward.

Mudrās which refer to something shining or sparkling (the mudrā for "shining," for "jewel," for "flowing water") will show both hands, or one hand, wide open, fingers spread, executing a vibrating or fluttering movement. Often the eyes move quickly from side to side, increasing the impression of "sparkling." The mudrā for "burning" or "fire" involves a similar vibrating movement of the hands as they travel upward, but the eyes contrive to suggest "danger," the lower lids being rapidly contracted and released, many times.

There are some interesting variations on the hand pose karttarī mukham. The same gesture, using this hand pose at the height of the waist, means "time" and "nearby." A variation, involving a circling from the wrist, but still waist-high, means "person" — evidently derived from the wearing of the muṇṭu which is tucked at the waist and which is the usual dress in Kerala. The same gesture, including the circular movement, but near the forehead, means "man."

Another gesture can mean "father," "uncle," or "teacher." This is an expression of the Kerala system of marumakattāyam or matrilineal descent in which the uncle or kāraṇavan is actual head of the household; it also expresses the concept of the teacher as father. A variation of this gesture means "son" and another variation "truth." In these mudrās the left hand is held in front of the center chest; the right circles it, rises to "ballet fifth high" and turns from palm up to palm down. The hand pose used in each instance signifies which meaning is intended.

HAMSA PAKṢA

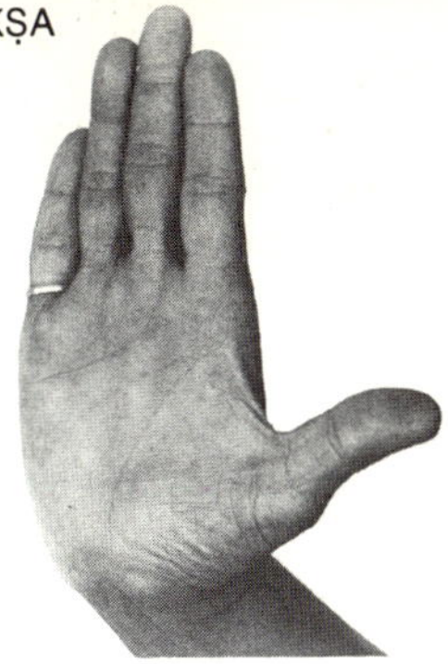

PATĀKA

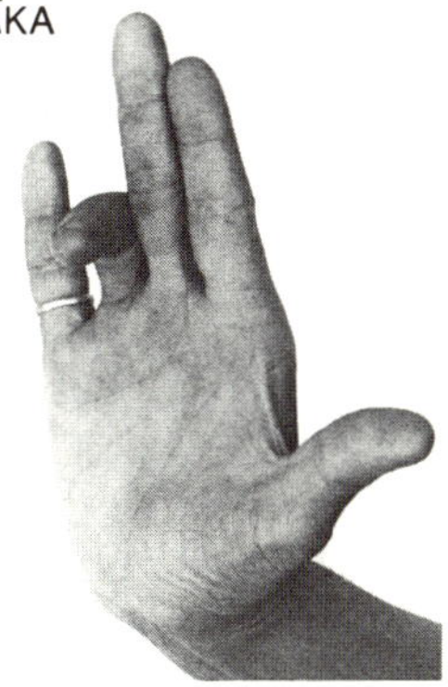

VARDHAMĀNAKA

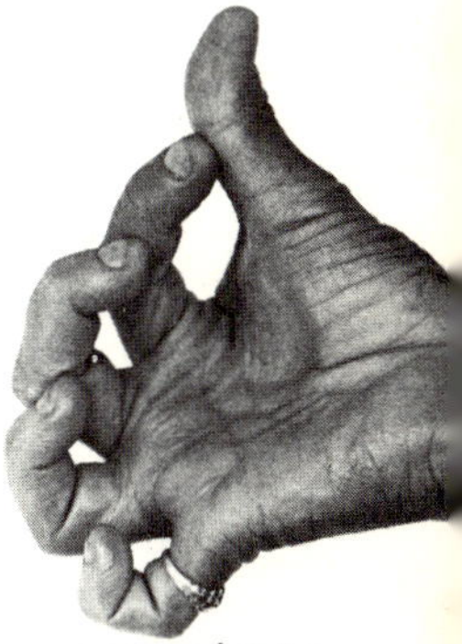

BHRAMARA

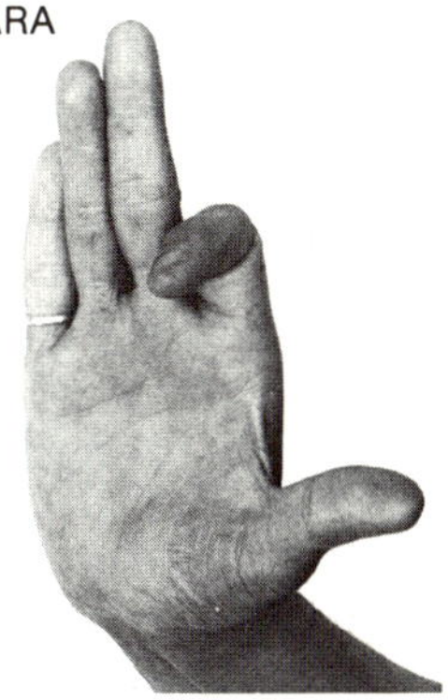

SARPAŚIRAS

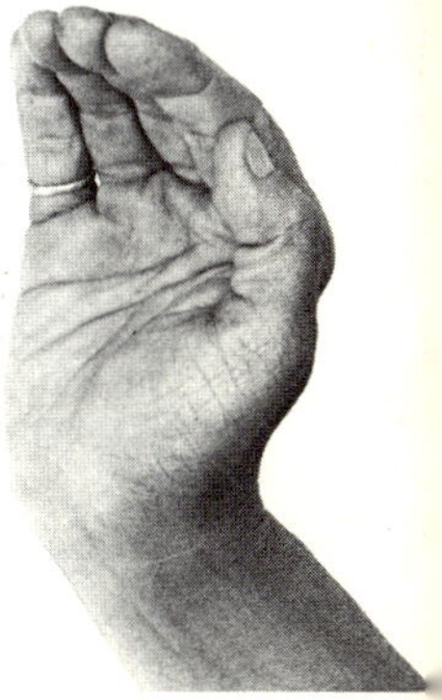

PALLAVA

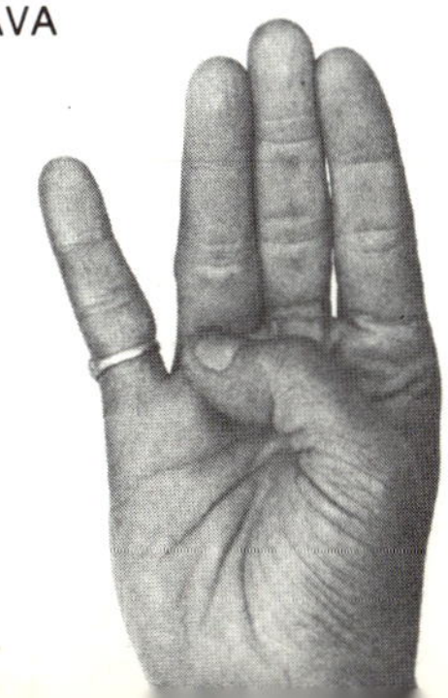

Another "set" of gestures — and the first "set" learned by the student — denotes the principal deities. They all begin from the hand pose añjalī (hands clasped as in prayer, but elbows bent outward) in "fifth high"; the body bends from the upper chest to the left, forward, and then comes center to a normal position as the hands open to a position even with the shoulders, forearms extended toward the audience and a little up. The hand pose held in each hand denotes which deity is shown.

Many mudrās have both a long and a short form. Others (such as for the negative, first and second person pronouns, etc.) have various forms depending upon the bhāva of the scene and also the character using them and the character addressed.

The acknowledged text used in Kathakaḷi for mudrās is the Hastalakṣaṇadīpika, the same text used for mudrās in Kūṭiyāṭṭam. That the mudrās of these two forms are closely related can be readily seen, although there are many variations, no doubt resulting from the separate developments of these two dramatic forms. In the Hastalakṣaṇadīpika each hand pose and its formation are described, and there follows a long list of the words for which this hand pose may be used. There is no further clue as to how the hand pose is used to give each of these meanings. Thus, the text itself means little without the living tradition as handed down from teacher to student.

The learning of the stylized facial expressions for the nine bhāvas is an important part of the training. Each is meticulously learned and practiced under the exacting eye of the teacher. It is also made clear to the student that he must learn to feel each bhāva as he portrays it; the stylized expression alone is far from adequate. In actual practice one bhāva may be modified by another; each scene has a sthāyibhāva or "permanent, basic" bhāva; it may also have a subordinate bhāva or sañcāribhāva. For example the bhāva of rati (the erotic) may have a sañcāribhāva of utsāha (heroism). Vismaya (wonderment) may have a sañcāribhāva of rati. There may be also other variations — the bhāva of śoka (compassion) need not be of the same type and degree in every case. The unfolding of the story in the most dramatically satisfying manner is all-important; the bhāvas in their basic form are tools which the actor must use with taste and discrimination.

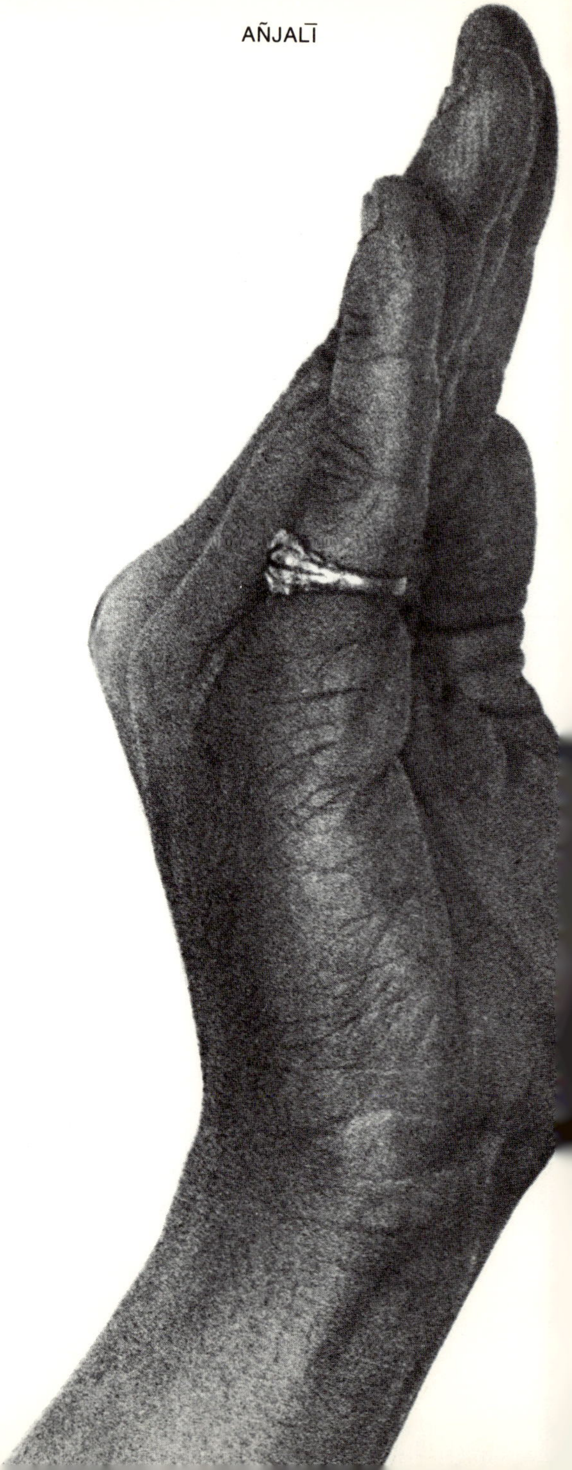

AÑJALĪ

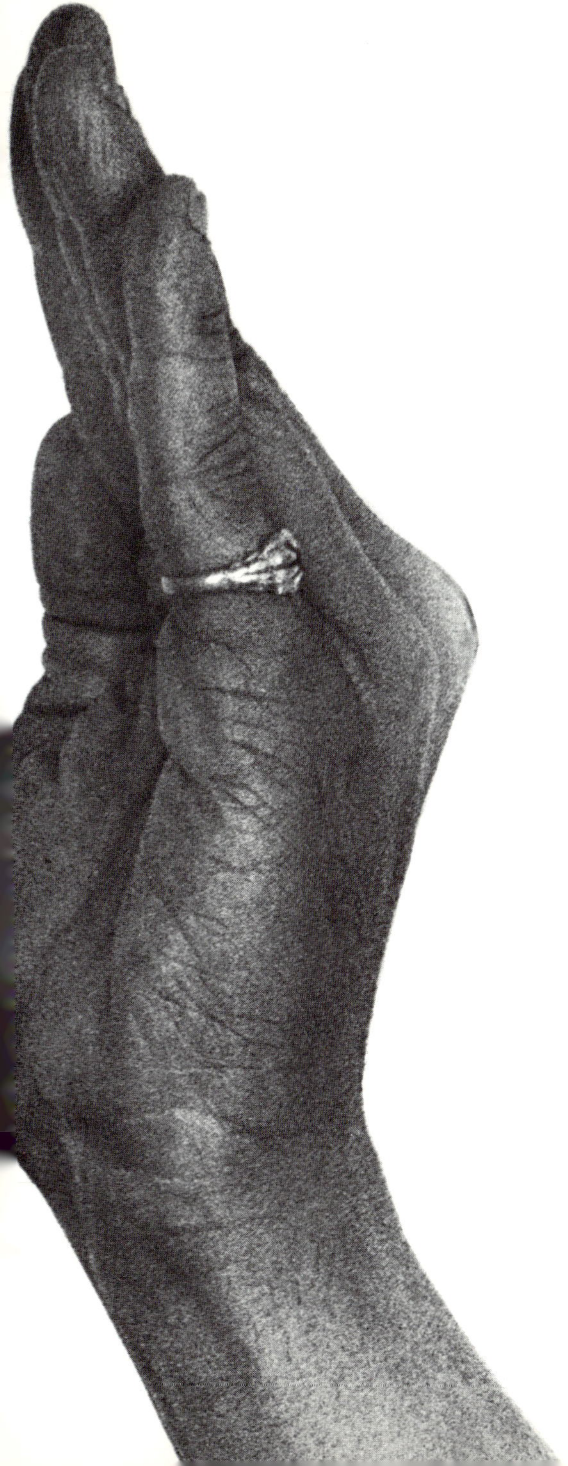

MṚIGAŚĪRṢA

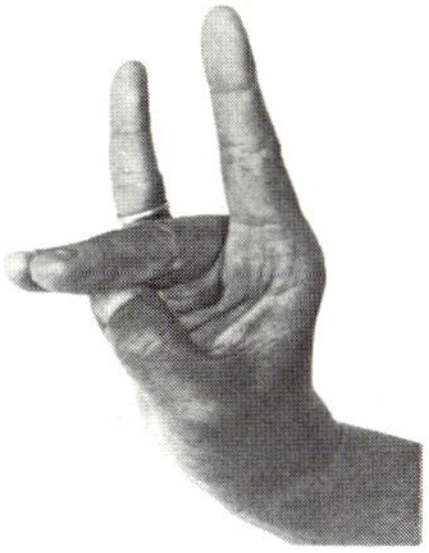

ŚIKHARA

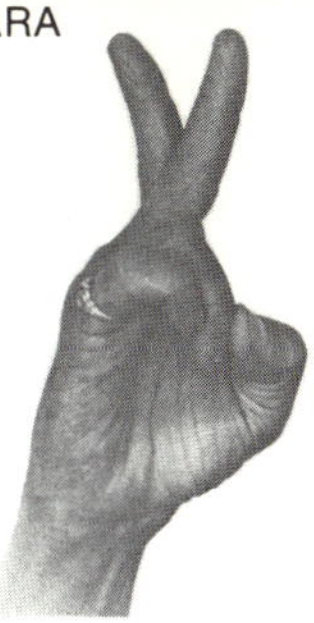

MUKURA

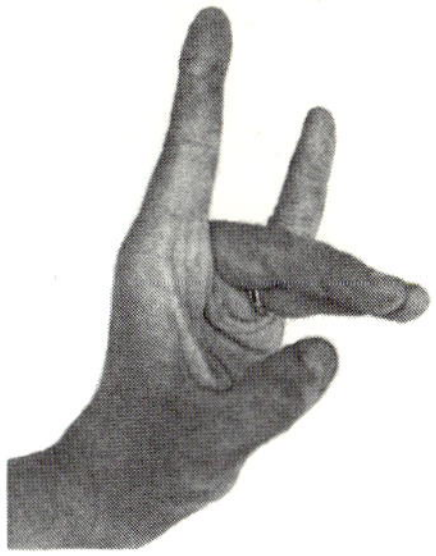

ARĀLA

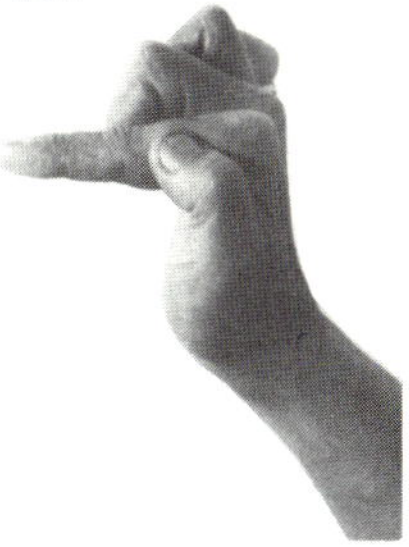

MUKULA

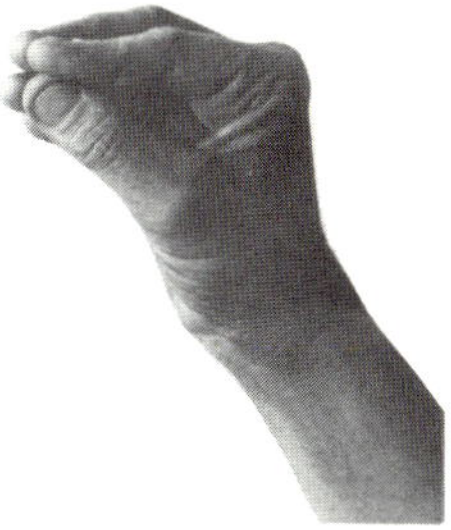

ŪRṆANĀBHA

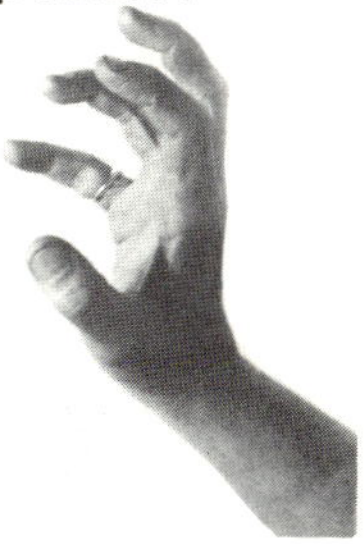

MUDRĀKHYA

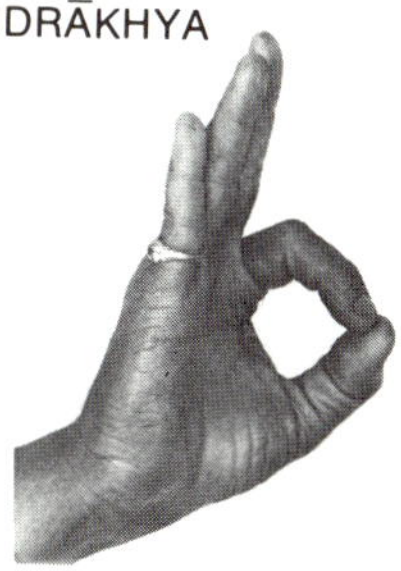

KAṬAKA

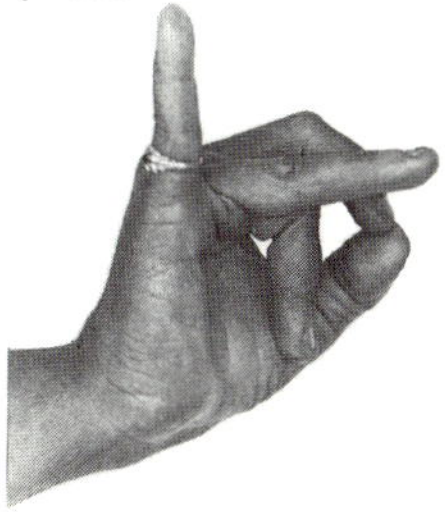

SŪCĪMUKHA

KARTARĪ MUKHA

ARDHACANDRA

ŚUKATUṆḌA

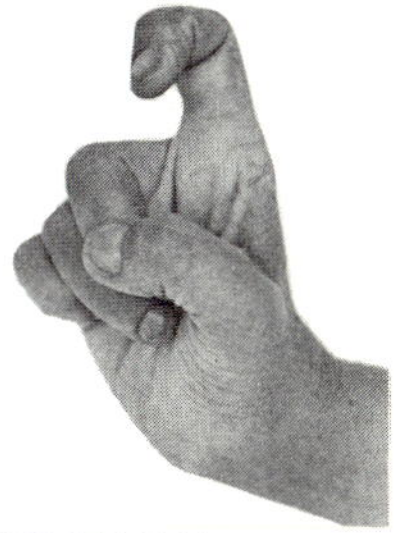

HAMSĀSYA

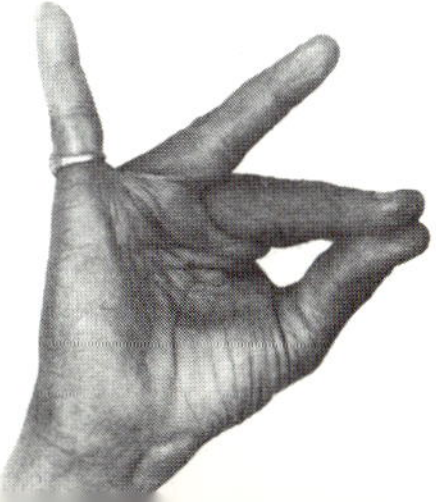

KAṬAKĀMUKHA

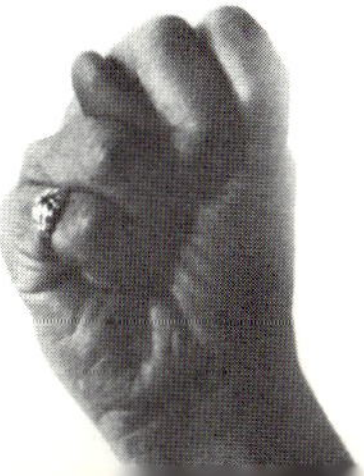

KAPITTHAKA

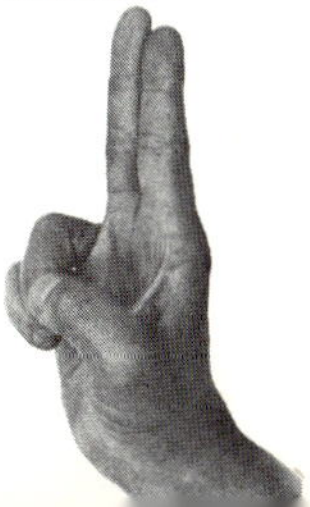

The Kathakaḷi student also learns three other stylized expressions: lajja (shyness), paribhavam (a kind of indignant contempt), and a special kind of krodha or anger. All three of these are used in female roles and in a male role when the actor imitates a woman. There are, as in the case of the nine bhāvas, several degrees and types of these, but one basic type of each is learned and practiced.

There are passages in Kathakaḷi wherein an actor "becomes" another person, or an animal or bird. An example of this is kēki nṛittam or "peacock dance." It is found in several of the stories and varies in the degree of elaboration. Usually it occurs in the course of a description of a scene; the text makes mention of peacocks in their "dance" and the actor imitates this dance. The movements of the body, hands, feet, eyes, head, combine to give the impression of the quick, proud, birdlike movements, the hands imitating the quivering and fluttering of the elaborate tail. When the text mentions an elephant, the actor "becomes" the ponderous but graceful beast, the left hand showing the trunk and the right the elephant's ear, waving slowly back and forth.

Another example of this convention is found in "Kalyāṇa Saugandhikam" when Bhīma shows the interpolation "Ajagarakabaḷitam," the story of an elephant attacked by a python and then by a lion (see synopsis of "Kalyāṇa Saugandhikam"). The actor "becomes" each of these creatures; first he is the elephant, tearing branches from the trees in his path. Then he becomes the python as he grasps the elephant's leg; then he is the elephant struggling to free himself from the python's grasp. Next he is the lion, sniffing the air to locate the source of the scent, finding and attacking the elephant. The entire episode is clearly depicted with an incredible degree of verisimilitude.

In "Bāli Vijayam" Rāvaṇa has a famous interpolation in which he "becomes" Śiva and also Pārvatī. It is particularly interesting to see a male actor, wearing the highly stylized and rather bizarre makeup and resplendent and very masculine costume of the katti, suddenly become the lovely Pārvatī, on her way to the river for her bath. And he is showing us, not exactly Pārvatī, but Pārvatī as seen through the eyes of Rāvaṇa; it is Rāvaṇa's impression of Pārvatī. Her femininity is exaggerated in the manner of one who uses a falsetto voice to imitate a woman rather than a voice pitched like that of an actual woman. Pārvatī and her companions play about in the water, wash and arrange their hair, modestly adjust their dress. Later, in a fit of pique because Śiva has in her absence been engaging in amorous play with the River Goddess, Gaṅgā, Pārvatī gathers up her children, Subrahmaṇya and Gaṇapati, and prepares to leave her unrepentant husband. The actor is Śiva; he is Pārvatī; he is himself, Rāvaṇa, showing his own part in the story or commenting upon it.

Such "stories within stories," of which the classic example is the Mahābhārata itself, are the very life-blood of Kathakaḷi. It is in these iḷakiyāṭṭams, as these interpolations are called, that the actor reaches the peak of his art and transforms himself — even his features — through that mysterious alchemy which is the essence of theatre.

In Kathakaḷi every single detail is designed to tell the story in the most effective way, to emphasize dramatic values, and to produce in the audience that rasa which is so much discussed in Indian dramatic theory. The great attention to detail, and the focusing of all these details toward the desired result, which we may call rasānanda, is the central core of this most perfect of dance-drama forms. Tāla, along with rāga, kāla, and other aspects of the music, dance movement techniques, the use of mudrās, use of the face and particularly the eyes, the use of poetic alliteration in the sung text with sounds which may invoke and enhance the proper mood, and of course the high degree of stylization of costuming and makeup — each detail is fitted into the others to produce a highly complex and superbly theatrical mosaic. One may endlessly analyze the elements of Kathakaḷi. In the end it is an inescapable fact that it is the brilliance, the intuitive "magic" of the individual artists which brings the art to life.

THE LEGACY OF A GREAT TRADITION

Kerala Kalamandalam, the Kerala State academy of theatre arts, is the most famous of all the professional schools now teaching Kathakaḷi. It is to this institution and the men who built it and sustain it that a great debt of gratitude is owed by all who care about or enjoy the theatre arts of India.

The organization of a center for the performing arts in Kerala was first conceived by the late great poet Mahakavi Vallathol Narayana Menon. At a time when the indigenous traditional arts of Kerala were virtually ignored and discredited by the public at large, Mahakavi Vallathol had the vision of recovering and perpetuating these arts. Against apparently unassailable odds, the poet Vallathol and his friend Śrī Manakkulam Mukunda Raja Tampuran organized every resource possible to begin to build an institution that would make it possible to preserve and sustain the theatre arts of Kerala. It is now over forty years since the inauguration of Kerala Kalamandalam. Poet Vallathol from the very beginning began to form a nucleus of the very best masters of Kathakaḷi music, both instrumentalists and vocalists, as well as the very finest teachers and actors. Among the great artists of the period were the actors Kunchu Kurup and Koppan Nair, the singer Ganacharya Swami Bhagavatar, the great percussionist Venkkitccaswami, and the celebrated master and true doyen of Kathakaḷi actors and teachers, the late Śrī Pattikkantodi Ramunni Menon Āśān, who for many years headed the faculty. He was a man of rare insight and taste and the most exacting disciplinarian of his day. Ramunni Menon Āśān's development of the Kalluvazhi style and school of Kathakaḷi, and his many outstanding contributions to the development of choreography within the tradition, have found their fruition in the achievements of his pupils who are the living legacy of his total devotion to the art.

Vallathol, throughout his later years, lavished his time and attention on the examination and refinement of the interpretation of the literature of Kathakaḷi. As a poet with a vast background in both Malayalam and Sanskrit, he brought to bear his knowledge of Puranic source material and poetic allusion in enriching the art and its interpretation and presentation. With the Āśāns, the masters of the art, he continually discussed and reexamined the past and present tradition and contributed greatly to the renaissance of Kathakaḷi.

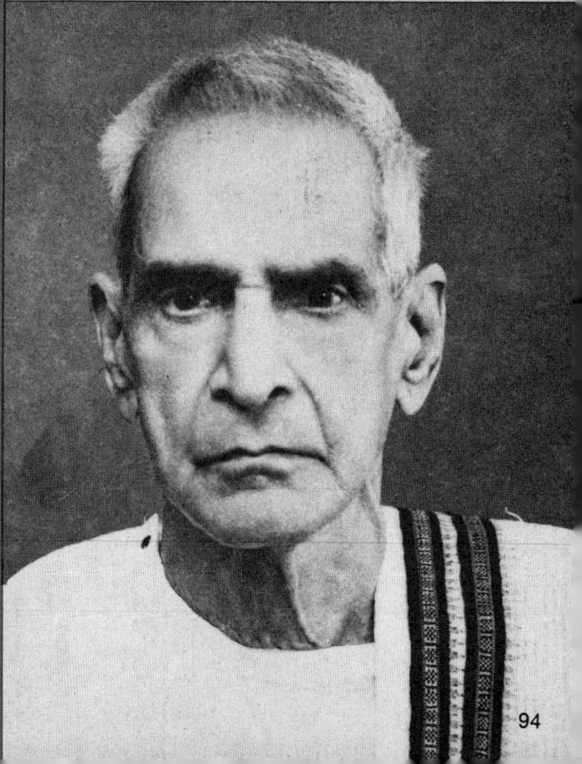

Kathakaḷi as an art is a generic form. It has several schools, two major varieties being distinctive. These are the northern and the southern schools within each of which there are variant individual schools often identified with a single personality and his disciples and his disciples' disciples. In middle Kerala, in the southernmost part of old Malabar, is the school called the Kalluvazhi sampradāyam, which is now identified with Kerala Kalamandalam and two smaller institutions, the P. S. Variar Kathakaḷi Yōgam and the Gandhi Sadhanam Kathakaḷi Yōgam. The evolution and change necessary to the life of a performing art have best been represented by these three centers. A disciple of Ramunni Āśān now heads each of these schools, and it is from these schools primarily that the finest actors and musicians have come forth in the past thirty years. The methods of change, the analysis of the technique, the form of the art, and the philosophical base from which to make valid changes in the tradition are the subject of a great part of the unpublished writing of Ramunni Āśān. Clearly one of his most significant contributions to the specific area of the method and philosophy of change is that it must be made within the tradition, can only validly be made within the tradition itself. His point of view is possibly a clue to the process of any valid change, adjustment, or transformation of traditional theatre art in India. The amateur mentors and self-appointed advisors in the arts everywhere in the world who stand outside the professional field, can never make use of the insight or understanding that only the trained professional within the art form can have. The exceptions to this rule are not unknown, but they are rarities of the first order. The excellence of discipline and high standard of technique established by Ramunni Āśān, and carried on by his best disciples, will be the only possible means of keeping the art of Kathakaḷi from the disaster that may overtake the careless popularization and subversion of so many traditional arts in India when control has been taken out of the hands of the professional artists who created them. What one sees on the stages of India, Europe, the Far East, and the Americas is still a genuine, authentic traditional art when Kerala Kalamandalam performs.

Much has been written about the continuities of traditional art. The confrontation of a changing society, changing systems of values, economic patterns, and education, are pressures brought to bear upon the life or death of many of India's cultural treasures. The methods of approach to the problem of inevitable change are many, and whatever may be the vagaries of the quality of the emerging, transforming product, change it must.

In the past the vocations of actor, singer or drummer were largely circumscribed by caste and community. Traditionally, certain groups from among the Nambūtiri, Ambalavāsi and Nāyar communities had mainly been the sources of personnel for other developed art forms as well as for Kathakaḷi. In the modern period this has been changed considerably and training is open freely to all strata of society. There have been several notable exceptions, but the pattern remains essentially the same: the students with the best aptitude often come from the same traditional social and cultural backgrounds as in the past. Even so, many who are trained, many who show marked ability, never continue their careers and tend to drift into other professions. The few who persist are invariably among the very best, and for the best there is always a future. In the future there is still a potential for a further development of the living tradition.

Today the art of Kathakaḷi is making the mercifully slow but dangerous transition from its original function as a socio-religious art form operating within the traditional culture, to the modern commercial theatre stages of the cities of not only Kerala and India, but the world at large. This is a transition that has already begun to produce a "secondary form" in the changing, still artificial, world of the emerging new order of uncertain values that tends to dominate popular patronage today in India. The transition is far from totally accomplished. The magnificent moments often attained by Kathakaḷi troupes performing on the stages of the Far East, Europe and the Americas are never quite the same as those realized within the traditional cultural context of Kathakaḷi's genesis and early development. They cannot be. All traditional arts in a changing society undergo certain transformations: one by one their cultural context, function and purpose are dislocated and they are transformed into something quite other than what they were before, never to be quite as they were. This can be a positive evolution; more often it is not. The first demands direction with great insight and intellectual perception; the second is too often the result of meaningless, tasteless, popularization and a total lack of perception by the changing patronage.

The tradition of Kathakaḷi is still very much alive. It has so far fared well in the hands of a few determined men for whom the goal is still, that rare thing, the perfection of the art rather than its exploitation. We are fortunate to be able to see such a tradition in the upward curve toward its apogee. While we may not all be able to experience that certain special atmosphere a theatre art can create when it is performed totally within and as a part of the fabric of its own social and cultural continuum, we can know something of it. We can sense, in the curtained dark artificial infinity of the modern stage, the rustle of invisible palm trees, the jewel points of fireflies and stars and the soft earth-scented breeze from an indigo sea. By some minor miracle, Kathakaḷi is a theatre of imagination. What you bring to this art you will receive back a hundredfold. The price of entry is the effort of awareness.

The reward is a heightened unfolding perception of a world never before imagined, a theatre world magically, vibrantly, remarkably alive. The vigorous survival of Kathakaḷi dance-drama as a major expression of traditional Indian literature and art, bridging the transformations of the past into the changing present, is perhaps the simplest proof of its timeless reality.

FOOTNOTES

1. Manomohan Ghosh (ed. and tr.) The Nāṭyaśāstra Ascribed to Bharata-Muni. Calcutta: The Royal Asiatic Society of Bengal, 1950, 1961. 2 vols. with companion vols. giving Sanskrit text. Revised 2d ed. of vol. I, Calcutta: Granthalaya Private Limited, 1967.
2. Tiruvangattu Narayanan Nambishan (ed.) Hastalakṣaṇadīpika. Kozhikode: K. R. Brothers, 1958.
3. C. Kunchu Nair, "The Kathakali and the Dance-Drama of India." The Unesco Courier, December 1967, p. 39.
4. Cerppattu Acyuta Varyyar and V. K. Sridharan Unni, eds. Āṭṭakathakaḷ. Quilon: S. T. Redyar and Sons, 1954 and 1956. 2 vols. There are many other published editions as well.
5. Manomohan Ghosh (ed. and tr.) Nandikeśvara's Abhinayadarpaṇam. Calcutta: Firma K. L. Mukhopadhyay, 1957, v. 37, p. 46 and p. 85.

105

abhinaya — The art of representation. In Indian dramatic theory there are four kinds of *abhinaya: āṅgikābhinaya,* representation by means of movement (gestures, pantomime, facial expression, etc.); *vācikābhinaya,* acting through the voice (speaking, chanting, singing); *āhāryābhinaya,* representation by means of costumes, ornaments, makeup; *sāttvikābhinaya* (q.v.), acting through the realistic expression and projection of emotion. (See Ghosh, *Nandikeśvara's Abhinayadarpaṇam,* v. 38-41, p. 46 and p. 86. Also Ghosh's translation of *The Nāṭyaśāstra Ascribed to Bharata-Muni,* Vol. I, Chapter VIII, v. 1-9, pp. 150-151.)

Ajagarakabaḷitam — A set interpolation often used in the Kathakaḷi dance-drama "Kalyāṇa Saugandhikam." In this interpolation Bhīma describes an episode which he sees while travelling through the forest in search of the *saugandhikam* flower. An elephant is attacked by a python and then by a lion; the story is shown in gesture and pantomime.

alaṅkāra — Ornamentation, elaboration, embellishment.

alarcca — Inarticulate vocal sounds of various sorts appropriate to particular characterizations in a Kathakaḷi dance-drama.

anibaddha — Not tied, free; without strict rhythm.

aṇiyaṟa — The dressing room, makeup room.

añjalī — One of the twenty-four basic hand poses of Kathakaḷi; in its double-hand form, it is the gesture of respect.

anupallavi — The second line of a *padam.*

Arjuna — The third Pāṇḍava brother. See Pāṇḍavas.

Āśān — The honorific title of a master of Kathakaḷi acting, music, or costuming and makeup.

aṭakkam — A choreographic passage used as an addition to the *valiya kalāśam.*

aṭanta — A *tāla* or rhythmic pattern of fourteen *mātras.*

āṭṭakatha — Literally, the "acted story." Refers to the specially written poetic text of a Kathakaḷi dance-drama.

Balabhadra — The elder brother of Kṛṣṇa. His symbols are a plough and a battle mace. In Kathakaḷi Balabhadra is shown as *pazhuppu veṣam.*

"**Bāli Vijayam**" — "The Victory of Bāli," a Kathakaḷi play based on an incident referred to in the *Rāmāyaṇa.*

Ballava (Valalan) — The name assumed by Bhīma in the thirteenth year of exile of the Pāṇḍavas. For a full year they were to remain incognito. Each of the five brothers and their wife Draupadī entered the service of Virāṭa, the King of Matsya. Bhīma became a cook in the royal kitchens under the name of Ballava.

Bhadrakālī — A Goddess of horrific form, summoned by Śiva to destroy the sacrifice of Dakṣa in the Kathakaḷi drama "Dakṣa Yāgam." Bhadrakālī is a *ṭeppu veṣam.*

Bhagavad Gītā — An ethical and religious poem of India, which appears in the *Mahābhārata.* It is widely available in English translation, including a Harper Torchbooks paperback edition (*The Bhagavad Gītā*, translated and interpreted by Franklin Edgerton. New York: Harper and Row, 1964). The Kathakaḷi scene in the "Mahābhārata" or "Pūrṇa Bhārata" was specially written for Kathakaḷi, but based on the original text.

Bhāgavata Purāṇa — A Sanskrit text of perhaps the ninth or tenth century which recounts legends and myths of Kṛiṣṇa. Many of these myths are charmingly retold in W. G. Archer's *The Loves of Krishna in Indian Painting and Poetry*. New York: Grove Press, Inc., n.d.

bhajanam (bhajan) — The group singing of devotional hymns.

bhakti — Devotion.

bhāva — Root sentiment or emotion. According to Indian dramatic theory there are nine basic emotional states or *bhāvas*, each with its corresponding *rasa*. The *bhāva* is the emotional state as experienced and projected by the actor; the *rasa* is the corresponding sentiment as perceived and experienced by the audience. The *Nāṭyaśāstra* lists eight of each; the ninth *bhāva* and ninth *rasa* are added in later texts such as Dhanamjaya's *Daśarūpa*. See Ghosh's translation of *The Nāṭyaśāstra Ascribed to Bharata-Muni*, Vol. I, Chapters VI and VII, pp. 100-125. Also, George C. O. Haas (tr. and ed.), *The Daśarūpa*. Delhi: Motilal Banarsidass, 1962, Chapter IV, v. 43-87, pp. 124-146.

Bhīma (Bhīmasena) — The second eldest of the Pāṇḍava brothers. See Pāṇḍavas.

bhrāntan — "Mad"; the phrase "Kathakaḷi *bhrāntan*" is a counterpart of the term "balletomane."

bhūtas — The goblins who form the army of the God Śiva.

Cākyār — The community whose hereditary profession is acting in Kūṭiyāṭṭam, the living Sanskrit drama tradition in Kerala.

cāmaram — The long false hair worn by Kathakaḷi actors.

campa — A *tāla* or rhythmic pattern of ten *mātras*.

campaṭa — A *tāla* of sixteen *mātras*.

caraṇams — The verses of a *padam*, three or more in number, following the *pallavi* and *anupallavi*.

ceṅṅalam — A circular bronze gong about eight inches in diameter which the *ponnāni* holds in the left hand and strikes with a stick to mark the accented beats of the rhythmic pattern.

ceṇṭa — Vertical cylindrical drum used in Kathakaḷi.

cevippūvu — "Ear flowers"; circular ornaments worn just above the ear in line with the eyes; worn for most male roles in Kathakaḷi.

colliyāṭṭam — Set choreography for some seventeen dance-dramas. The stories having *colliyāṭṭam* are considered to be the most classical of the Kathakaḷi repertoire. The term also means "rehearsal."

coriṭṭukai — A composed percussion composition for *śuddha maddaḷam;* part of the overture for a Kathakaḷi drama.

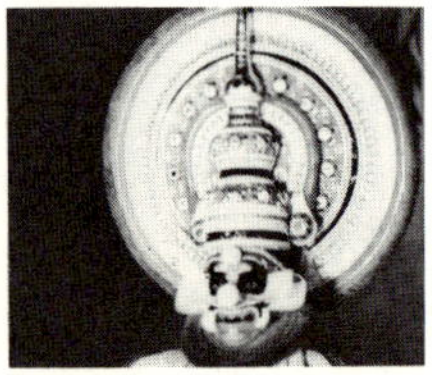

cukannattāṭi — "Red beard"; also called *cuvannattāṭi* and *connuttāṭi*. One of the character types of Kathakaḷi; the demonic and villainous anti-hero in whom the quality of *tamas* predominates. The *cukannattāṭi* makeup and costume are also worn by some animal characters such as Bāli and Sugrīva of the Vānaras (forest animals, monkeys).

cuṇṇam — Calcinated shell lime; one of the ingredients of the white paste used in the *cuṭṭi*. Used also in making the finger stalls worn by the *śuddha maddaḷam* player.

cuṇṭappūvu — A tiny seed-like object from the plant *solanum pubescens*. The *cuṇṭappūvu* when put into the eye induces a rose-red coloring of the white of the eye. It is used for all roles in Kathakaḷi; for some roles more than one *cuṇṭappūvu* is used to intensify the color.

cuṭṭi — The decorative white paper and paste border framing the makeup. There are several variant forms of *cuṭṭi.*

cuṭṭi tuṇi — A tied head band worn as a frame for the makeup and to support the headdress of the actor.

cuzhippu — A set series of choreographic motifs that form one aspect of the dance movement in Kathakaḷi.

daṇḍakam — A variety of verse and meter employed in the sung poetic text for Kathakaḷi. Sung in *anibaddha* style without percussion accompaniment, the *daṇḍakam* is a descriptive introduction or interlude.

dhanāśi — The concluding benediction in choreographic form, accompanied by song and percussion instruments, which completes the Kathakaḷi dance-drama. It is to be performed only by an auspicious character, usually a *pacca.*

dharma — Duty, justice, law, order.

Draupadī — Daughter of Drupada, King of the Pāñcālas; wife of the five Pāṇḍava brothers. At one time the Pāṇḍavas and their mother Kuntī were living as Brāhmaṇas and concealing their identities after escaping from a trap set for them by Duryodhana. Being in the Pāñcāla country, the brothers attended the *svayamvara* of Princess Draupadī. Of the assembled suitors, only Arjuna was able to accomplish the extremely difficult feat devised by King Drupada, and thus won Draupadī in marriage. When they returned to the hut where they were living, their mother Kuntī, thinking they had returned as usual with alms gathered from the townspeople, told them that they must share among them what they had received that day. Thus Draupadī became the wife of all five brothers. It seems that polyandry was rare in ancient India, although apparently polygamy was a common practice.

"Duryodhana Vadham" — "The Destruction of Duryodhana," a Kathakaḷi play based on the *Mahābhārata,* ending with the death of the leader of the Kauravas.

gada — A battle mace, the special weapon of Bhīma.

Gaṇapati (also called Gaṇeśa) — The elephant-headed God who is the second son of Śiva and Pārvatī, and whose chief function is to overcome obstacles. It is considered auspicious to worship him before any undertaking.

ghats — The mountains and hills forming a barrier and dividing the Deccan plateau from the southern coast of India.

Gīta Govinda — A religious poem in Sanskrit, intended to be sung; written by Jayadeva, twelfth century. The *Gīta Govinda* deals with stories of Kṛṣṇa and the milkmaids. Among the English translations is one by George Keyt. *(Śrī Jayadeva's Gīta Govinda.* Bombay: Kutub-Popular Pvt. Ltd., 1940.)

guṇa — Quality or attribute. According to one of the concepts of Indian philosophical thought, the three universal qualities are *sattva* (goodness or virtue), *rajas* (passion, violence), and *tamas* (darkness, ignorance).

hamsa — Variously interpreted as a gander, a swan, or a mythical bird. The *Hamsa* in the Kathakaḷi "Naḷa Caritam, First Day's Story" is usually referred to in English as a Golden Swan.

hasta — "Hand"; often used to mean one of the twenty-four basic hand poses used in gesture; also may refer to the meaningful gesture itself which involves two or more of the basic hand poses. The word is used interchangeably with *hastamudrā* or simply *mudrā*.

iḷakiyāṭṭam — "Moving-acting"; refers to interpolations in the drama, and also to dance movements which accompany specific gestures.

ilattāḷam — Bronze metal cymbals for keeping time, played by the second singer.

iṭantala — The "left head" or top of the *ceṇṭa* (drum). It is the *iṭantala* which is usually played in Kathakaḷi, the *valantala,* "right head" or bottom being played only for special scenes where a deity reveals his cosmic form, etc. (To play the *valantala,* the drummer tips the drum so that the *valantala* is to his right.)

iṭekka — An hour-glass shaped drum which can be made to sound all the notes of the scale; used in Kathakaḷi along with the *śuddha maddaḷam* for *padams* enacted by female characters.

kāl sādhakam — Exercises of rhythmic structure for the legs and feet.

kāla — Tempo.

kaḷari — The military gymnasium; the gymnasium where Kathakaḷi training takes place.

kalāśam — The decorative dance passages which occur in Kathakaḷi generally between the lines of a *padam;* also dance passages used for entrances. There are in addition *kalāśams* which are not danced at all, but which are played on the percussion instruments and function as "signals."

kaḷi viḷakku — The special lamp of bronze used for lighting the drama from ancient times.

Kalluvazhi — A village in Central Kerala. The Kalluvazhi *sampradāyam* is the tradition of Kathakaḷi to which Pattikkantodi Ramunni Menon Āśān belonged and the tradition which is followed at Kerala Kalamandalam.

"Kalyāṇa Saugandhikam" — The title of a Kathakaḷi play based on the incident of "The Divinely Fragrant Flower" from the *Mahābhārata.*

kāraṇavan — The maternal uncle; head of the family in the *marumakattāyam* or matrilineal family system in Kerala.

kari — One of the character types in Kathakaḷi; a demoness whose character expresses the distasteful or horrific as well as the slightly comic.

Kārkkōṭakan — A serpent which appears in "Naḷa Caritam, Second Day's Story." Naḷa rescues Kārkkōṭakan from fire, but is bitten for his pains. Kārkkōṭakan then explains that the effect of the poisonous bite will serve as a disguise until the time is right for Naḷa to resume his own identity. A *ṭeppu* character of Kathakaḷi.

karuttatāṭi — "Black beard"; a character type similar to the *cukannattāṭi* except that black is predominant in the makeup and costume.

Kāṭṭāḷan — "Forest man"; the character of aborigine hunter or jungle dweller. The disguise adopted by Śiva in the drama "Kirātam."

Kāṭṭāḷatti — "Forest woman"; the wife of Kāṭṭāḷan. The disguise adopted by Pārvatī in "Kirātam" and one of the *ṭeppu* characters of Kathakaḷi. The actor has a degree of freedom in the makeup pattern; usually black, green, or dark blue predominates in the makeup and costume.

katti — "Knife"; one of the character types of Kathakaḷi. The quality of *rajas* predominates in this character. *Katti* roles are among the most interesting in Kathakaḷi because the *katti* has both noble and ignoble qualities. For instance, although Duryodhana, the eldest of the Kauravas, was self-centered and treated the Pāṇḍavas unfairly, he had great courage and fulfilled his duties as a Kṣatriya or member of the warrior class; for this reason the Gods showered fragrant flowers upon him as he died in battle.

Kaṭuttatāṭi — The character type to which Kāṭṭāḷan belongs.

Kauravas — In its broader sense the term refers to the descendants of King Śantanu of the Kuru race, which includes the Pāṇḍavas as well as their cousins and bitter enemies, the one hundred and one sons of Dhṛitarāṣṭra, the blind king. Most commonly, however, the term is used to mean the latter of whom Duryodhana is the eldest and Duhśāsana the second.

kēki nṛittam — Interpolation in the form of a descriptive and imitative dance of the peacock.

kēḷikkoṭṭu — The special drumming performed at sunset announcing the performance of Kathakaḷi on the same evening.

kēśabhāra kirīṭam — The crown worn by divine, noble, or royal characters (*pacca, katti,* and certain *pazhuppu* and *tēppu* characters), having a nimbus-like circular attachment at the back.

"Kīcaka Vadham" — "The Destruction of Kīcaka," a Kathakaḷi play based on a story from the Virāṭa Parva of the *Mahābhārata.*

"Kirātam" — "The Forest Hunter," title of a Kathakaḷi play based on an episode from the Āraṇyaka Parva of the *Mahābhārata.* A *kirātan* is a member of a tribe of mountain people.

kuṇḍala — Large convex circular "earrings" worn with the *kirīṭam.*

Kuntī — The mother of the three eldest Pāṇḍavas, Yudhiṣṭhira, Bhīma, and Arjuna; stepmother of the twins, Nakula and Sahadeva, whose mother was Mādrī, the co-wife of Kuntī.

Kūṭiyāṭṭam — "Combined acting"; refers to the Sanskrit theatre tradition preceding the development of Kathakaḷi. Kūṭiyāṭṭam is the art of the Cākyār and Nambyār communities.

lalita — The form of a wantonly beautiful woman assumed by a demoness for evil purposes.

Mahābhārata — The longest epic poem in any language and the source of the stories for many Kathakaḷi dramas; the story of the great war on the battlefield of Kurukṣetra between the Pāṇḍavas and their cousins the Kauravas, the events leading to that war and its aftermath. The *Mahābhārata* contains a great many episodes and myths only indirectly connected with the main story, as well as discourses on religion, government, philosophy, etc. A retelling of the main story may be found in Chakravarthi V. Narasimhan's *The Mahābhārata.* New York: Columbia University Press, 1965. No. LXXI of the series Records of Civilization: Sources and Studies.

Malayalam (Malayāḷam) — A Dravidian language; the language spoken in the State of Kerala.

Mālinī — Female garland-maker; the name which Draupadī took during the thirteenth year of exile when she and her Pāṇḍava husbands were supposed to conceal their identities. Draupadī became a maid-servant of the wife of Virāṭa, King of Matsya. She took service as a *sairandhrī*, which signifies a domestic servant. Her duties were to dress the queen's hair, make garlands, and grind the fragrant sandalwood paste.

Maṇipravāḷam — A literary language with several variants combining Sanskrit and Malayalam.

manōdharmma — "Imagination"; improvised passages of interpolation; the discretionary choice by the actor of interpolation.

marumakattāyam — The tradition of inheritance through the female line peculiar to some social groups in Kerala.

mātra — A unit of time in the system of *tālas* or rhythmic patterns.

Mēḷappadam — One of the compositions which form the prelude to the dance-drama, performed by the musicians.

minukku — "Shining"; a makeup type of Kathakaḷi, in which the face is painted a matte creamy yellow, then dusted with mica; used for more naturalistic characters (women, sages, Brāhmaṇas, royal messengers, etc.).

mṛidaṅgam — A double-headed barrel-shaped drum more widely used in Tamilnad.

mudrā — "Sign"; see *hasta*.

mukhābhinaya — The representation of emotional mood through facial expression.

muṇṭu — The two or four yards cloth worn in Kerala; it is wrapped about the waist and tucked, and reaches to the ankles.

muṟiyaṭanta — A *tāla* of six *mātras*.

muṭi — A vase-like silver decorated crown, fringed at the top with peacock feather tips; worn by incarnations of Viṣṇu.

Nakula — One of the Pāṇḍava brothers. Nakula and his twin Sahadeva were the youngest. See Pāṇḍavas.

"Naḷa Caritam" — "The Story of Naḷa," a Kathakaḷi play of four parts, intended to be presented on four successive nights. The play is based on one of the subsidiary stories found in the *Mahābhārata.*

nāmam — "Name"; the sectarian mark worn on the forehead by devotees of Viṣṇu, a stylized form of which is a part of the makeup of *pacca* characters of Kathakaḷi.

neṯṯi bandham — "Forehead tie"; a black band decorated with silver beads worn on the forehead as a part of the Kathakaḷi ornaments.

nōkku — "Look"; a lowering of the *tiraśśīla* so that the audience has a partial view of the actor or actors before their first full appearance.

pacca — "Green"; a makeup type in Kathakaḷi in which the face is painted a rich green color; used for noble, virtuous, and heroic characters in whom the quality of *sattva* is dominant.

padam — A vocal compositional form widely used in South Indian music, with *pallavi, anupallavi,* and *caraṇams.* Those portions of the poetic text of Kathakaḷi which are sung with percussion accompaniment and enacted by the characters in gesture.

pallavi — The first line of a *padam,* recurring (in whole or part) after the *anupallavi* and after each *caraṇam,* functioning as a kind of refrain.

pañcāri — A *tāla* of six *mātras*.

Pāṇḍavas — The five heroes of the *Mahābhārata:* Yudhiṣṭhira, the eldest; Bhīma, the second son; Arjuna, the third son; and Nakula and Sahadeva, the twins. Owing to a curse, their legal father, Pāṇḍu, was prevented from begetting offspring. Each of the Pāṇḍavas was the son of one of the deities with the aid of a boon bestowed upon Kuntī, one of the two wives of Pāṇḍu, by the sage Durvāsa. Kuntī was the mother of Yudhiṣṭhira (by Yama, God of death and dharma), Bhīma (by Vāyu, the wind God), and Arjuna (by Indra, King of the Gods). She instructed Mādrī, her co-wife, in the magic spell and enabled her to conceive the twins, Nakula and Sahadeva, by the Aśvins, the twin deities of dawn and twilight. Pāṇḍu was the younger brother of the blind King, Dhṛitarāṣṭra, father of the Kauravas. The rivalry between the Pāṇḍavas and Kauravas began in their childhood and culminated in the great war which is the main event of the *Mahābhārata.*

pati — Slow; *pati kāla* or *patiññakāla* is a very slow tempo used in *patiññāṭṭampadams* in Kathakaḷi.

patiññāṭṭampadams — The very slow and highly classical *padams* used in Kathakaḷi for romantic love scenes and for other scenes where the leisurely tempo is appropriate to the emotional mood portrayed. Primarily for *pacca* or *katti* characters and having usually only four lines of text, these *padams* will be one hour in duration.

pazhuppu — "Ripe"; a makeup type found in Kathakaḷi and in Kūṭiyāṭṭam. The face is a gleaming reddish golden color. In Kathakaḷi this makeup is worn by actors playing Brahmā, Śiva, Balabhadran, etc.

ponnāni — The first or lead singer who plays *ceṅṅalam.*

Purāṇa — Ancient; ancient story or legend. A class of sacred works containing religious instruction as well as history and mythology.

Puṟappāṭu (Muzhuva and Pakuti) — "The going forth"; danced prelude before the first act of the drama begins. *Muzhuva* means "complete"; *pakuti* means "half." Pakuti Puṟappāṭu, the shorter version, was composed within the last twenty years and is to be performed by only two characters, Kṛiṣṇa and his brother Balabhadra. The longer version may be performed by other *pacca* characters and by female characters, representing heroes or deities and their wives or consorts.

"Pūrṇa Bhārata" — "Full or complete *Mahābhārata,*" comprising selected scenes from several of the Kathakaḷi dance-dramas on *Mahābhārata* themes to make one connected story.

puṣpaka vimāna — The aerial chariot in which Rāvaṇa carried Sītā off to Laṅkā.

rāga — Having to do with the melodic aspect of Indian music, the *rāga* has been variously defined by musicologists. The lack of a similar concept in present-day Western music presents difficulties of terminology. Two decisive elements are the use in a specific *rāga* of only certain notes of the scale and of certain varieties of musical ornamentation.

Rāmanāṭṭam — The eight plays based on the story of the *Rāmāyaṇa* which form the earliest literature of Kathakaḷi.

Rāmāyaṇa — The story of Rāma, son of King Daśaratha of Ayodhyā. Rāma was also the seventh *avatāra* or incarnation of Viṣṇu and was

born as a man to save the world from the dangerous and powerful Rāvaṇa. He exemplifies the ideal king as well as the faithful husband; his wife, Sītā, is the ideally devoted wife. A brief summary of the story may be found in A. L. Basham's *The Wonder That Was India.* (New York: Grove Press, Inc., 1954, pp. 412-413.) Ralph T. H. Griffith's translation of the text was published as Vol. XXIX of the Chowkhamba Sanskrit Studies series. (*The Ramayan of Valmiki.* Varanasi: Chowkhamba Sanskrit Series Office, 3rd ed., 1963.) The story is well loved in India and appears also in the dance-drama forms of Southeast Asia.

rasa — Pertains to the savor of aesthetic delight through the delineation of emotions and sentiments. *Rasānanda* is the blissful state of aesthetic delight, an expanded state of consciousness, ultimately an abstraction. See *bhāva.*

Sahadeva — One of the Pāṇḍava brothers. He and his twin, Nakula, were the youngest. See Pāṇḍavas.

śamkhu — The conch shell, used as a musical effect at important junctures in the drama.

samnyāsin — An ascetic; one who has renounced the world.

sampradāyam — A tradition or traditional learning, descending from teacher to pupil.

sañcāribhāva — A subordinate emotional state which follows, supports, or modifies the main emotion in a dramatic situation.

sandhya — Union, juncture, especially of day and night; morning and evening twilight, an auspicious time for religious observances.

śaṅkiṭi — The second singer who plays bronze cymbals and supports the first singer.

sāttvikābhinaya — "Truth in acting, the true essence of acting"; the rare and genuine emotional quality as projected by the actor, sometimes shown by involuntary states such as blushing, turning pale, fainting, tears, paralysis, horripilation, etc. See Ghosh's translation of *The Nāṭyaśāstra Ascribed to Bharata-Muni,* Vol. I, Chapter VII, v. 93-106, pp. 145-147.

Śilappadikāram — "The Story of the Jewelled Anklet"; a narrative poem in Tamil, probably from about the fifth century A.D. Two English translations are available, one by V. R. Ramachandra Dikshitar (*Śilappadikāram.* Madras: Humphrey Milford, Oxford University Press, 1939) and the other by Alain Danielou (*Shilappadikaram; The Ankle Bracelet.* New York: New Directions, 1965).

śilpa śāstras — The canons and treatises on the arts and architecture.

ślokam — A metrical verse used for purposes of description between scenes in the drama, sung in *anibaddha* style.

sōpāna — "Stairs"; in Kerala the style of singing for ritual and dramatic purposes is known as the "*sōpāna* style."

sthāyibhāva — "Lasting or permanent state of mind"; the dominant emotion in a dramatic sequence.

"Subhadrā Haraṇam" — "The Abduction of Subhadrā," a Kathakaḷi play based on an incident in the *Mahābhārata.* The story relates how Subhadrā, the sister of Kṛṣṇa and Balabhadra, was carried off by Arjuna to be his bride.

Subrahmaṇya — The God of war, also called Skanda; the elder son of Śiva and Pārvatī.

Sudarśana Cakra — Viṣṇu's discus, a sharp circular missile weapon.

śuddha maddaḷam — The barrel-shaped double-headed drum used for all *padams* in Kathakaḷi.

Śūrpaṇakhā — The demoness sister of Rāvaṇa in the *Rāmāyaṇa.* Her name means "having fingernails like winnowing fans."

svaras — Here referring to the tonal recitation schemes used in Kūṭiyāṭṭam, the living Sanskrit drama of Kerala.

svayamvara — "Self-choice"; the custom whereby in ancient and medieval India a girl of the Kṣatriya community was allowed to choose her husband. Sometimes the father of the girl devised a difficult feat of strength or valor; he among the assembled suitors who performed this feat in the most creditable manner won the hand of the girl in marriage. She presented a garland to the husband-elect to signify the choice.

tāla — Rhythmic pattern. In Kathakaḷi there are six *tālas: campaṭa, aṭanta, campa, tripuṭa, muṟiyaṭanta,* and *pañcāri.* The number of *mātras* in the *tāḷavaṭṭam* and the arrangement of accented beats distinguish one *tāla* from another.

tāḷavaṭṭam — One complete cycle of the *tāla.*

Tantrik — Refers to the magico-religious techniques of ritual worship. The tradition employs methods and calculations exploiting symbolism, numerology, astrology, mathematics, and the manipulation of sound.

taṟavāṭu — The ancestral residence or lineage.

tāṭi — "Beard"; there are three main varieties of "bearded" characters in Kathakaḷi, distinguished not only by the color of the beard but also by the makeup, the ornaments, and the costume.

tāyambaka — A percussion composition which is a prominent feature of temple festivals. Although it is now performed also on other percussion instruments, the classic *tāyambaka* is by one lead *ceṇṭa,* four accompanying *ceṇṭas,* and two or more *ilattāḷam.*

tēppu — "Painted"; a class of characters in Kathakaḷi. The term embraces a large variety of characters, some of which appear in only one drama. The actor is allowed some freedom in the makeup.

tiranōkku — "Curtain-look"; an entrance device involving manipulation of the *tiraśśīla* and a choreographed passage of movement and acting (with variations) which builds suspense before the first full appearance of *katti, cukannattāṭi, kari* characters, etc. (not used for *pacca* or *minukku*).

tiraśśīla — The colorful Kathakaḷi curtain held by two men. A rectangular cloth usually about six feet by nine feet, it is used to separate the scenes of the drama and for entrances and exits.

tōṅkāram — A choreographic passage with several varieties, appearing in connection with a *valiya kalāśam.* A line of text is often sung during the *tōṅkāram* and the gestures for that line are shown.

Tōṭayam — An item of pure or abstract dance, traditionally a part of the preliminaries before the dance-drama. Seldom included in the performance today, it is still an important part of the training and *kaḷari* practice.

tripuṭa — A *tāla* of seven *mātras.*

turn-out — A term common in classical ballet and other forms of dance to denote the stance or position in which the knees are turned outward. The perfect or ideal "180° turn-out" means that the legs are rotated outward from the hips so that the knees are completely to the sides.

valantala — "Right head" (of a drum). See *iṭantala.*

vana varṇṇana — "Description of the forest." An interpolation customarily found in "Kalyāṇa Saugandhikam"; Bhīma describes the forests and mountains which he traverses in his search for the *saugandhikam* flower.

vandana ślokas — Songs in praise and invocation of the deities.

veḷḷattāṭi — "White beard"; a Kathakaḷi character type; the makeup and costuming of Hanumān, the divine monkey-devotee of Rāma.

vēṣam — Role; the assumed personality and costume, etc., of a character in a drama. The character types, as *pacca vēṣam, katti vēṣam, strī vēṣam* (female role), etc.

yōgam — An assembly; here it means an organization or troupe. Traditionally the Kathakaḷi Yōgam is an all-male organization.

Yudhiṣṭhira — The eldest of the Pāṇḍava brothers. See Pāṇḍavas.

A NOTE ON THE AUTHORS

Clifford R. Jones and his wife, Betty True Jones, have studied art history and theatre in India for a number of years since 1959. The difficult task of providing a text with accurate basic information about a complex theatre art, in brief concise form, has been theirs. A considerable body of further historical, descriptive, and comparative work on the theatre forms of South Asia by the authors is forthcoming. Both of the authors have a professional background in dance and theatre and have continued to study the practical technique of Kathakaḷi first-hand at Kalamandalam; thus they are able to write from a very close point of view. Dr. Jones's research and study were made possible by Fellowships and Grants from the Fulbright Program in India, 1959-61; the Ford Foundation, 1961-62; and the American Institute of Indian Studies, 1965-66, 1968-69. Mrs. Jones received Grants from the Fulbright Program in India in 1965-66, and from the American Philosophical Society, 1968-69. Dr. Jones is Assistant Professor of South Asian Art History and Theatre in the South Asia Regional Studies Department, University of Pennsylvania. Mrs. Jones is Lecturer in Theory and Technique of Indian Classical Dance, College of General Studies, University of Pennsylvania.

Jan Steward is Art Director and Photographer on the staff of the American Society for Eastern Arts. Author of the visual design and illustration, Mrs. Steward has provided the visual images that again and again span the challenging distance between information and experience. Her photographic record was made in Kerala on a special trip to India under the auspices of the American Society for Eastern Arts in 1969.

kathakali kathakali kathaka